TECHNICAL REPORT

T0302543

The Bankruptcy Abuse Prevention and Consumer Protection Act of 2005

Evaluation of the Effects of Using IRS Expense Standards to Calculate a Debtor's Monthly Disposable Income

Stephen J. Carroll, Noreen Clancy, Melissa A. Bradley, Jennifer Pevar, Marianne Culhane, Michaela White

Prepared for the Executive Office for U.S. Trustees

RAND INSTITUTE FOR CIVIL JUSTICE

The research described in this report was prepared for the Executive Office for U.S. Trustees by the RAND Institute for Civil Justice.

Library of Congress Cataloging-in-Publication Data

The Bankruptcy Abuse Prevention and Consumer Protection Act of 2005 : evaluation of the effects of using IRS expense standards to calculate a debtor's monthly disposable income / Stephen J. Carroll ... [et al.].
p. cm.
Includes bibliographical references.
ISBN 978-0-8330-4183-8 (pbk. : alk. paper)
1. United States. Bankruptcy Abuse Prevention and Consumer Protection Act of 2005. 2. Bankruptcy—United States—Accounting. 3. Debtor and creditor—United States. 4. Income tax deductions for expenses—United States. I. Carroll, Stephen J., 1940–

KF1539.B36 2007
346.7307'8—dc22

2007021207

Published 2007 by the RAND Corporation
1776 Main Street, P.O. Box 2138, Santa Monica, CA 90407-2138
1200 South Hayes Street, Arlington, VA 22202-5050
4570 Fifth Avenue, Suite 600, Pittsburgh, PA 15213-2665
RAND URL: http://www.rand.org/
To order RAND documents or to obtain additional information, contact
Distribution Services: Telephone: (310) 451-7002;
Fax: (310) 451-6915; Email: order@rand.org

Preface

One of the main changes that the Bankruptcy Abuse Prevention and Consumer Protection Act of 2005 (BAPCPA) introduced was the requirement that certain debtors filing for bankruptcy use IRS expense standards for certain expense categories rather than their current expenses to calculate their monthly disposable income (MDI). The RAND Corporation conducted qualitative and quantitative analyses to estimate the effect of using the IRS standards on debtors and to determine whether using this standard is having an effect on bankruptcy courts.

This research was sponsored by the Executive Office for U.S. Trustees (EOUST), the mission of which is to promote the integrity and efficiency of the U.S. bankruptcy system. This report should be of interest to state and federal policymakers concerned with bankruptcy issues. It should also be of interest to practitioners involved in the bankruptcy system and to the credit industry.

The RAND Institute for Civil Justice

The mission of RAND Institute for Civil Justice (ICJ) is to improve private and public decisionmaking on civil legal issues by supplying policymakers and the public with the results of objective, empirically based, analytic research. ICJ facilitates change in the civil justice system by analyzing trends and outcomes, identifying and evaluating policy options, and bringing together representatives of different interests to debate alternative solutions to policy problems. ICJ builds on a long tradition of RAND research characterized by an interdisciplinary, empirical approach to public policy issues and rigorous standards of quality, objectivity, and independence.

ICJ research is supported by pooled grants from corporations, trade and professional associations, and individuals; by government grants and contracts; and by private foundations. ICJ disseminates its work widely to the legal, business, and research communities and to the general public. In accordance with RAND policy, all ICJ research products are subject to peer review before publication. ICJ publications do not necessarily reflect the opinions or policies of the research sponsors or of the ICJ Board of Overseers.

Information about ICJ is available online (http://www.rand.org/icj/). Inquiries about research projects should be sent to the following address:

Robert T. Reville, Director
RAND Institute for Civil Justice
1776 Main Street
P.O. Box 2138
Santa Monica, CA 90407-2138
310-393-0411 x6786
Fax: 310-451-6979
Robert_Reville@rand.org

Contents

Tables

Executive Summary

One of the main changes introduced by the Bankruptcy Abuse Prevention and Consumer Protection Act of 2005 (BAPCPA) was the requirement that certain debtors filing for bankruptcy use IRS expense standards for certain expense categories rather than their current expenses to calculate their monthly disposable income (MDI). This change can affect both the options available to a debtor considering filing for bankruptcy and the amount the debtor must pay to creditors under a repayment plan.

In this RAND Corporation study, we assessed the effects of this change on debtors and the courts. We conducted the research in three steps: First, we reviewed the case law to identify relevant issues; second, we conducted interviews and focus groups with those involved in the bankruptcy process to understand background and context; and third, we examined samples of bankruptcy cases filed in eight judicial districts to estimate the effects of using the IRS standards to calculate a debtor's MDI.

Effects on the Courts

BAPCPA took effect too recently for appellate courts to have had time to settle the many open questions. Because there is considerable lack of uniformity among judicial districts in application of the IRS standards in chapters 7 and 13 of the Bankruptcy Code, similarly situated debtors may have substantially different payment obligations depending on the jurisdiction in which they live.

Most judges report that each bankruptcy case now requires more of their time, but the effects seem to vary greatly depending on the district. The increase in workload is not attributable to any particular provision of the new law; therefore, what portion may be due to the IRS expense standards is not known.

Results of Analysis of Bankruptcy Cases

Fraction of Chapter 7 Cases Using the IRS Standards

About 7 percent of the Chapter 7 debtors in our samples had above-median incomes, but their deductions, including those calculated using IRS standards, resulted in MDIs that met the Chapter 7 criteria. The percentage of debtors who filed for Chapter 7 even though their incomes exceeded the applicable median varies considerably across the country. We have no data on the extent to which the IRS standards, as part of the means test, may have deterred debtors from filing under Chapter 7.

Fraction of Chapter 13 Cases Using the IRS Standards

Slightly more than one-quarter of Chapter 13 debtors in our samples had above-median incomes and, consequently, were required to use the IRS expense standards to calculate their MDIs. Almost three-quarters of the debtors in our samples who filed under Chapter 13 had below-median incomes. These debtors presumably could have filed under Chapter 7 had they so chosen but opted for Chapter 13 filing instead.

There was substantial variation across judicial districts in the fraction of Chapter 13 filers whose incomes exceeded the median and, consequently, used the IRS expense standards in calculating their MDIs.

Effects of Using the IRS Standards in Calculating MDI

In every sampled district, the average deductions allowed under the IRS standards are considerably higher than the average equivalent deductions based on reported current expenses. Higher deductions result in lower MDIs. MDI is reduced by an average of $490 in all sampled districts combined when the IRS standards are used. In individual districts, the average reduction in MDI due to the use of the IRS standards ranges from $311 in the Middle District of Florida to $612 in the Northern District of Ohio. The IRS standards result in larger deductions, on average, and, therefore, lower MDIs across the country.

Effects of Specific IRS Standards

Two of the IRS standards primarily account for this differential. The IRS standards for living expenses and for transportation ownership are generally favorable to debtors. In every sample district, these IRS standards allow debtors deductions that exceed their reported current expenses. Conversely, in every sample district, the IRS standards for nonmortgage housing expenses and for vehicle operation and public transportation allow debtors lower deductions than their reported current expenses. The IRS standard for mortgage or rental expenses generally favors owners, though the differences between the deduction that owners are allowed using the IRS standards and their current expenses in that category generally are not large. The effects on renters of using the IRS standards for mortgage or rental expenses are mixed. In five of the eight sample districts, using the IRS standards results in smaller deductions, on average, than does using current rental expenses. In the other three districts, the IRS standard rental allowance exceeded, on average, the debtors' current rental expenses.

Effects of Using the IRS Standards on Different Types of Debtors and in Different Districts

Using IRS standards to calculate deductions benefits the average homeowner more than it does the average renter, but the difference is small, about $65 per month. Among homeowners and among renters, the only other significant difference in the effects of the IRS standards on different types of debtors is for debtors with high current incomes. In general, higher-income debtors gain less using the IRS standards rather than their current expenses than do otherwise similar, lower-income debtors. For homeowners, the average difference in deductions calculated using the IRS standards rather than current expenses is about $70 lower for each additional $1,000 in current monthly income. For renters, the average difference in deductions calculated using the IRS standards rather than current expenses is about $175 lower for each additional $1,000 in current monthly income. This effect is significant for homeowners and highly significant for renters. Debtors' assets, liabilities, and expenditures were not significantly related to the effects of using the IRS standards in calculating their deductions.

The results for the eight judicial districts examined suggest that, controlling for debtors' financial characteristics, there are some systematic differences among the districts in the effects of using the IRS standards instead of the corresponding current expenses to calculate a debtor's MDI. The district effect is more pronounced for homeowners than for renters.

Acknowledgments

The authors would like to thank the students and library staff at Creighton University School of Law who assisted in our collection of Chapter 13 filing data. Special thanks go to Laura Pfeffer, who led the effort, but we are also grateful to Troy Johnson, Nicholas Coleman, Kevin Cruz, Stacy Jo Ferrel, Rita Trumble, Tony Vandenbosch, Liz Culhane, Jonathan Wegner, and Jeff Coolman. We would also like to thank several RAND colleagues. Katie Smythe assisted in conducting interviews and provided useful feedback on drafts of this report. Christopher Beighley and Amelia Haviland designed and conducted the empirical analyses of the data extracted from the bankruptcy case samples. Comments by our reviewers, Elaine Reardon of RAND and Katherine Porter of the University of Iowa College of Law, increased the quality and clarity of this report.

Abbreviations

AO	Administrative Office of the U.S. Courts
BAPCPA	Bankruptcy Abuse Prevention and Consumer Protection Act of 2005
BLS	Bureau of Labor Statistics
C.D. Cal.	Central District of California
D. Utah	District of Utah
E.D.N.Y.	Eastern District of New York
EOUST	Executive Office for U.S. Trustees
ICJ	RAND Institute for Civil Justice
IQR	interquartile range
M.D. Fla.	Middle District of Florida
MDI	monthly disposable income
N.D. Ohio	Northern District of Ohio
S.D. Iowa	Southern District of Iowa
SMSA	standard metropolitan statistical area
USTP	U.S. Trustee Program
W.D. Tenn.	Western District of Tennessee
W.D. Tex.	Western District of Texas

CHAPTER ONE

Introduction

On April 20, 2005, President George W. Bush signed the Bankruptcy Abuse Prevention and Consumer Protection Act of 2005 (BAPCPA). Most provisions of the act took effect October 17, 2005. One of the main changes that BAPCPA introduced was the requirement that debtors filing for bankruptcy whose monthly income exceeds the median income for their household size in their state (*above-median–income debtors*) use the IRS expense standards for certain expense categories rather than their current expenses to calculate their monthly disposable income (MDI). MDI is the amount of money that debtors presumably have available to pay their general, unsecured debts after their expenses, including payments on secured and priority claims, are deducted from their income.

A debtor's calculated MDI can affect whether he or she can seek a discharge of all dischargeable debts under Chapter 7 of the Bankruptcy Code or must, instead, file a plan for repaying at least a portion of those debts under Chapter 13 of the Bankruptcy Code. The repayment amount is determined by the debtor's calculated MDI. As a consequence, the use of the IRS expense standards in calculating a debtor's MDI can affect both the options available to a debtor considering filing for bankruptcy and the amounts that the debtor must pay monthly to creditors under a Chapter 13 repayment plan.

The U.S. Congress required the Executive Office for U.S. Trustees (EOUST) to examine the effects of the IRS standards on debtors and the bankruptcy courts (Public Law 109-8, §103[b][1]). The statute reads as follows:

> (1) IN GENERAL.—Not later than 2 years after the date of enactment of this Act, the Director of the Executive Office for United States Trustees shall submit a report to the Committee on the Judiciary of the Senate and the Committee on the Judiciary of the House of Representatives containing the findings of the Director regarding the utilization of Internal Revenue Service standards for determining—
>
> (A) the current monthly expenses of a debtor under section 707(b) of title 11, United States Code; and
>
> (B) the impact that the application of such standards has had on debtors and on the bankruptcy courts.

EOUST, in turn, asked RAND to help it address these questions by estimating the effects on debtors and the bankruptcy courts of using the IRS standards. RAND conducted qualitative and quantitative analyses to assess the effects of using the IRS standards to calculate a debtor's MDI. We reviewed the case law to identify those issues surrounding the use of the IRS expense standards that were ending up in the courts. We also conducted interviews and group discussions with informed individuals and government employees involved in the bankruptcy process to elucidate issues and patterns. Finally, we examined samples of bankruptcy cases filed in eight judicial districts to empirically estimate the effects of using the IRS standards to calculate a debtor's MDI. This report presents the results of these analyses.

Background

The bankruptcy process is governed primarily by Title 11 of the U.S. Code, known as the Bankruptcy Code, and by the Federal Rules of Bankruptcy Procedure. Bankruptcy proceedings are supervised by and litigated in the U.S. bankruptcy courts, a part of the U.S. district court system. There are two basic types of personal bankruptcy filings:

- liquidation under Chapter 7 of the Bankruptcy Code
- rehabilitation of the debtor under Chapter 13 of the Bankruptcy Code.[1]

Individual debtors whose debts are primarily consumer debts may file for a discharge of all their dischargeable debts[2] under Chapter 7 of the Bankruptcy Code if their monthly income is less than the median family income for their household size in their state. Above-median–income debtors[3] may also file under Chapter 7, but they must satisfy a means test to avoid a presumption that their case should be dismissed. Specifically, above-median–income debtors are presumed to be filing abusively under Chapter 7 if their 60-month disposable income, calculated using the IRS expense standards, is greater than $10,000 or, if less than $10,000 and greater than $6,000, is more than 25 percent of their total, nonpriority, unsecured debt.[4] In the first year of BAPCPA, U.S. trustees filed motions to dismiss in three-quarters of the presumed abuse cases that did not voluntarily dismiss or convert, and they declined to file motions in about a quarter of such cases (White, 2006).

[1] The Bankruptcy Code also provides for filings under Chapter 11, which allows businesses and individuals in certain circumstances to pay debts while continuing to operate, and under Chapter 12, which allows eligible family farmers and fishers to continue operating while reorganizing business affairs.

[2] Certain categories of debts (e.g., alimony and child support obligations, student loans, tax arrears, government fines and penalties) will not be discharged in a Chapter 7 bankruptcy.

[3] To simplify this discussion, we use the phrase *above-median–income debtor* to refer to a debtor whose income exceeds the median family income for his or her household size in his or her state.

[4] The U.S. trustee to whom a case is assigned may challenge a filing because it does not meet the requirements for filing under Chapter 7. The debtor may withdraw the filing or dispute the U.S. trustee's finding, in which case the bankruptcy judge will decide whether the filing will be accepted. For cases filed on or after April 1, 2007, the amounts will increase per 11 USC §104.

Accordingly, the use of the IRS expense standards to calculate MDI can affect whether above-median–income debtors will be eligible to file for a discharge of all their dischargeable debts under Chapter 7. Below-median–income debtors who file under Chapter 7 are not affected by the use of the IRS expense standards.

A debtor in Chapter 7 must turn over all nonexempt property to a trustee who will sell the property and distribute the proceeds to the debtor's creditors.[5] Below-median–income debtors who wish to retain property that would have to be surrendered in Chapter 7 may file under Chapter 13 of the Bankruptcy Code. Under Chapter 13, the debtor must repay a portion of debts through a court-approved repayment plan of three to five years. The IRS expense standards do not affect below-median–income debtors who file under Chapter 7 or Chapter 13.

Above-median–income debtors who file under Chapter 13, either voluntarily or because they do not meet the Chapter 7 means test, must pay a court-approved portion of their debts through a three-to-five–year repayment plan. However, because their monthly income is above median, their repayment plan is based on their projected MDI calculated as the difference between their monthly income and their allowable expenses under the IRS expense standards. The use of the IRS expense standards will affect such filers to the extent that the standards affect their calculated MDIs.

IRS Expense Standards

The IRS has developed expense standards to decide how much a delinquent taxpayer should have to pay the IRS each month to repay back taxes on an installment basis.[6] BAPCPA requires above-median–income debtors to calculate their MDIs using the IRS expense standards rather than their current expenses (Bankruptcy Code, §707[b][2][A][ii]). The IRS standards apply to five categories of expenses:

- living expenses (e.g., food, clothing, household supplies, personal care, and miscellaneous)
- nonmortgage housing and utility expenses (e.g., utilities, repairs, and maintenance)
- mortgage or rental expenses
- vehicle operation and public transportation expenses
- transportation ownership and lease expenses.

The allowance for living expenses depends on the debtor's income and family size, irrespective of where the debtor lives.[7] The two allowances for housing (nonmortgage housing and utility expenses and mortgage or rental expenses) each depend on the debtor's family size

[5] Each state has laws that determine which items of property, in what amounts, are exempt in bankruptcy.

[6] The IRS standards were originally designed for use in the areas of installment agreements and offers in compromise, whereby a delinquent taxpayer seeks to work out a tax deficiency with the IRS. The standards were not intended to apply in the areas of debt or eligibility under the Bankruptcy Code.

[7] The allowance for living expenses is slightly higher in Alaska and Hawaii.

and county of residence. The vehicle operation and public transportation expense allowance depends on whether the debtor owns zero, one, or two or more cars and varies by standard metropolitan statistical area (SMSA) or census region. The transportation ownership or lease expense allowance depends on whether the debtor owns or leases one or two cars. The amounts specified are national figures.

The IRS has determined the amount of the standard in each expense category. The Bankruptcy Code specifies the calculations that the debtor must make using the IRS standards. For example, the debtor is instructed to simply add the applicable IRS living expense standard to his or her deductions. But, to calculate his or her deduction for mortgage or rental expenses, the debtor subtracts his or her average monthly payment for any debts secured by the home from the applicable IRS mortgage or rental expense standard.

The use of the IRS expense standards in these five categories affects debtors' calculations of their MDIs. Debtors also deduct their current expenses in other expense categories (e.g., taxes, mandatory payroll deductions, life insurance, child care, and health care) in calculating their MDIs.

Research Questions

Our analyses of the effects of using the IRS expense standards to calculate a debtor's MDI focused on six questions:

1. How have court rulings affected the use of IRS standards in calculating a debtor's MDI, and to what extent has this use affected the bankruptcy courts' workload?
2. What fraction of Chapter 7 filers had above-median incomes but satisfied the Chapter 7 presumption because their MDIs, after allowed deductions, satisfied the means test?
3. To what degree did use of the IRS standards affect debtors who filed for Chapter 13?
4. For above-median–income, Chapter 13 filers, how does MDI calculated using current expenses compare with MDI calculated using IRS expense standards?
5. For above-median–income, Chapter 13 filers, what, if any, financial factors are systematically related to the difference between MDI calculated using current expenses and MDI calculated using IRS expense standards?
6. For above-median–income, Chapter 13 filers, do patterns in the differences between MDI calculated using current expenses and MDI calculated using IRS expense standards differ across judicial districts?

How Have Court Rulings Affected the Use of IRS Standards in Calculating a Debtor's MDI, and to What Extent Has This Use Affected Bankruptcy Courts' Workloads?

A number of questions of statutory interpretation of the IRS expense standards have been brought to the bankruptcy courts. On these, bankruptcy courts have frequently disagreed. BAPCPA took effect too recently for appellate courts to have had time to settle the many open questions. As a result, application of the IRS standards in chapters 7 and 13 is not uniform among federal judicial districts. We review the case law regarding aspects of BAPCPA in which judicial decisions have been most prominent. The need to address disputes regarding appropriate interpretation of BAPCPA has also increased the courts' workload. We review the available data on how BAPCPA has affected this workload.

What Fraction of Chapter 7 Filers Had Above-Median Incomes but Satisfied the Chapter 7 Presumption Because Their MDIs, After Allowed Deductions, Satisfied the Means Test?

We estimate the number of above-median–income debtors who filed for Chapter 7. Above-median–income filers who would have filed under Chapter 7 but found that their MDIs, calculated using the IRS expense standards, raised a presumption of abuse that they could not rebut either will have filed under Chapter 13 or never filed at all.[8] We have no way to determine the fraction of would-be Chapter 7 filers who, because of the effects of using the IRS standards, either filed under Chapter 13 or never filed at all. Consequently, we can only note the fraction of above-median–income Chapter 7 filers whose total deductions, including the IRS expense allowances, permitted them to pass the means test. We cannot estimate the fraction of would-be Chapter 7 filers who were affected by the use of IRS standards in the sense that they were precluded from filing under Chapter 7.

To What Degree Did Use of the IRS Standards Affect Debtors Who Filed for Chapter 13?

The IRS expense standards apply only to above-median–income Chapter 13 filers. In these cases, the IRS expense standards are used in calculating their projected MDIs for the purposes of establishing a repayment plan. The answer to this question quantifies the extent to which the use of IRS expense standards affects Chapter 13 filers, whatever may be the direction and magnitude of the effect.

For Above-Median–Income, Chapter 13 Filers, How Does MDI Calculated Using Current Expenses Compare with MDI Calculated Using IRS Expense Standards?

The answer to this question establishes the extent to which the use of the IRS standards by above-median–income Chapter 13 filers in calculating their deductions affects the amount of projected MDI. How does MDI calculated using the IRS standards compare with MDI calculated using debtors' current expenses? Are the differences between the two calculations generally in the same direction and on the same order of magnitude? If not, what is the distribution of the differences between the different calculations? Do some types of debtors, distinguished by their financial circumstances or where they file, generally have higher MDIs using one calculation than they do if using the other?

For Above-Median–Income, Chapter 13 Filers, What, If Any, Financial Factors Are Systematically Related to the Difference Between MDI Calculated Using Current Expenses and MDI Calculated Using IRS Expense Standards?

The answer to this question identifies the extent to which a debtor's financial circumstances (assets, liabilities, income, and expenditures) are systematically related to the effect of using

---

[8] Individual debtors with secured debts in excess of $922,975 or unsecured debts in excess of $307,675 are ineligible for Chapter 13 protection. They may seek a discharge under Chapter 11.

the IRS standards to calculate his or her MDI. The answer will identify whether some types of debtors tend to systematically gain, or lose, from the requirement that they use the IRS expense standards to calculate their MDIs.

For Above-Median–Income, Chapter 13 Filers, Do Patterns in the Differences Between MDI Calculated Using Reported Current Expenses and MDI Calculated Using IRS Expense Standards Differ Across Judicial Districts?

In both our quantitative and qualitative analyses, we will explore the consistency of results across different areas of the country. We will explore hypotheses about the factors that might cause any geographical differences in the qualitative analyses.

Research Approach

We conducted qualitative analyses based on interviews and group discussions with informed individuals, including government employees, involved in the bankruptcy process to elucidate issues and patterns. We also conducted empirical analyses of information from samples of Chapter 7 and Chapter 13 bankruptcy cases filed in eight judicial districts across the country.

Qualitative Analyses

Overall, we interviewed more than 70 individuals involved in the bankruptcy process (e.g., attorneys, trustees, consumer group members, judges) to get a broad view of how use of the IRS expense standards is affecting debtors and the courts. We conducted 26 individual interviews, one focus group, and discussion groups at four U.S. trustee regional offices.

Individual interviews were conducted by telephone. Participants were chosen from a variety of organizations. Many had played numerous roles in the bankruptcy process. Most individuals who participated had been working in the bankruptcy arena before the passage of BAPCPA. Therefore, they could provide insight into how the bankruptcy process has changed since the law was implemented and compare the old bankruptcy process to the current system. We did not interview debtors, as their information is limited to their one experience and not relative to other experiences or to how they might have fared pre-BAPCPA.

We sought to collect qualitative data that supported the analysis and were sensitive to specific subgroups within the population of participants but were not unduly influenced by a single region of the country. To this end, during a national convention of consumer bankruptcy law experts, we conducted a focus group discussion with eight private bankruptcy attorneys and one former bankruptcy attorney who now works for a consumer protection group. This allowed us to gather a geographically diverse sample of participants at a central location. We also conducted group discussions with approximately 40 staff members, including assistant U.S. trustees, staff attorneys, bankruptcy analysts, and paralegals, from four U.S. trustee regional offices in various geographic areas. The discussion guide used can be found in the appendix.

For the individual interviews, we used a general interview guide that highlighted subjects to be covered by the project staff. These interviews were not standardized, and the content and structure varied for each individual. Separate protocols were developed for the attorney focus group discussion and the U.S. trustee regional office group discussions.

Bankruptcy Case Samples

Data on the characteristics of personal bankruptcy cases are not available by judicial district. We asked the EOUST Office of Research and Planning to identify eight judicial districts that it considered representative of bankruptcy cases across the country. Based on its experience and knowledge of the various judicial districts, EOUST identified eight judicial districts that it believed offered a representative mix of urban and rural sites, size, relative frequency of Chapter 7 and Chapter 13 cases, and native versus foreign-born filers. Both prior to and after BAPCPA took effect, these eight districts accounted for approximately one-sixth of the individual bankruptcy cases across the country. These eight districts were thought to be fairly representative of all districts. The authors adopted these recommended districts as their sample districts. Table 1.1 lists the selected districts.

In consultation with EOUST, we determined that April 1, 2006, was a date sufficiently long after BAPCPA took effect that cases filed on, or soon after, that date are likely to reflect the effects of BAPCPA and would have effectively been completed by the time the sample was drawn in November 2006. We drew the first 50 Chapter 7 cases filed in each of the selected districts on or immediately after April 1, 2006, that had not been dismissed or converted to a Chapter 13 case by December 8, 2006. We also drew the first 100 Chapter 13 cases filed in each of the selected districts on or after April 1, 2006, by an above-median–income debtor that had not been dismissed or converted to a Chapter 7 case by December 8, 2006.

As we collected our Chapter 13 samples, we counted the number of Chapter 13 cases encountered in the process in which the debtor's income was below the applicable median income. This allowed us to calculate the fraction of Chapter 13 filings that survived roughly eight months without dismissal or conversion in which the debtors were not required to use the IRS expense standards.

Table 1.1
Judicial Districts Selected for Bankruptcy Case Samples

Judicial District	U.S. Trustee Program (USTP) Office Locations
Eastern District of New York (E.D.N.Y.)	Brooklyn and Central Islip
Western District of Texas (W.D. Tex.)	Austin and San Antonio
Western District of Tennessee (W.D. Tenn.)	Memphis
Northern District of Ohio (N.D. Ohio)	Cleveland
Southern District of Iowa (S.D. Iowa)	Des Moines
Central District of California (C.D. Cal.)	Los Angeles, Riverside, Santa Ana, Woodland Hills
District of Utah (D. Utah)	Salt Lake City
Middle District of Florida (M.D. Fla.)	Orlando and Tampa

We drew cases filed voluntarily by individuals, whether filing individually or jointly. We did not include filings by entities other than individuals.

When we combined the bankruptcy cases from all districts to obtain an estimate for all districts, we weighted the cases for each individual district by the total number of filings under the relevant chapter in that district between April 1 and September 30, 2006. Thus, a result for all sample districts with respect to some aspect of Chapter 7 or 13 filings reflects the distribution of Chapter 7 or 13 filings across the eight districts in the relevant period (April 1 through September 30, 2006). These weights range from approximately 1 to 10 across the districts and reflect the number of filings that each selected filing represents. By weighting the results by the sampling weights, the results here are representative of all the cases in these eight districts and, thus, one-sixth of the bankruptcy cases in the country. Because the districts included in our samples were selected to be representative of districts across the country, our results for all districts should be representative of bankruptcy cases, on average, across the country.

Organization of This Report

Chapter Two reviews the bankruptcy system. Chapter Three presents our analysis of the effects of the IRS expense standards on the bankruptcy courts. Our empirical analyses of the case samples and the resulting estimates of the effects of using the IRS expense standards on debtors are presented in Chapter Four. Chapter Five summarizes the results and presents our conclusions.

CHAPTER TWO

The Bankruptcy System

The bankruptcy process is governed primarily by Title 11 of the U.S. Code, known as the Bankruptcy Code, and by the Federal Rules of Bankruptcy Procedure. There are two basic types of bankruptcy filings:

- liquidation under Chapter 7 of the Bankruptcy Code
- rehabilitation or reorganization of the debtor under chapters 11, 12, and 13 of the Bankruptcy Code.

Chapter 7 Bankruptcy

A Chapter 7 bankruptcy debtor receives a discharge of all dischargeable debt in return for turning over all of the debtor's nonexempt assets to a trustee.[1] A debtor may be denied a discharge only on specified grounds, including fraud committed in the bankruptcy process. Specific debts are statutorily nondischargeable (e.g., certain tax debts, alimony, child support).

A debtor may file for Chapter 7 relief without regard to the amount of the debtor's assets, liabilities, or degree of solvency. However, the Bankruptcy Code now contains the means test, a hurdle to filing based on the debtor's level of MDI. Individual debtors whose debts are primarily consumer debts are subject to the means test. A debtor can be barred from Chapter 7 protection if (1) his or her gross income exceeds the median income for his or her household size in the state of residence and (2) his or her MDI after allowed deductions, including those based on the IRS standards, exceeds statutory amounts, because the debtor is presumed to have an ability to repay his or her debts. It is USTP's responsibility to review the debtor's disposable income calculation under the means test. If USTP finds that a debtor fails the means test, USTP will ask the court to dismiss the case. The court determines whether a debtor qualifies for Chapter 7 protection.

[1] Although bankruptcies take place in the federal court system and follow federal law, state law may affect the property that a debtor may exempt (e.g., equity in a personal home and contents). Section 522 of the Bankruptcy Code provides that, unless a state opts out, a debtor may use a federal list of exemptions found at section 522(d). Most, but not all, states have opted out and established a list of exemptions. Debtors in certain states may elect to use federal exemptions instead of state ones. Thus, for example, a Texas debtor may choose either the state list or the federal list.

If the trustee determines that there is nothing to be collected from the debtor and USTP determines that the means test is satisfied, then the case usually moves rapidly through the system and the debts are discharged. Historically, 70 percent of personal bankruptcies have been filed under Chapter 7.

Chapter 11 Bankruptcy

Chapter 11 of the Bankruptcy Code allows individual debtors and business entities to pay debts while continuing to operate. A Chapter 11 debtor, often with the participation of creditors, creates a reorganization plan allowing repayment of all or part of the debt.

Chapter 12 Bankruptcy

Chapter 12 of the Bankruptcy Code allows eligible family farmers and fishers to file for bankruptcy, reorganize business affairs, continue operating, and repay all or part of the debts.

Chapter 13 Bankruptcy

Under Chapter 13 of the Bankruptcy Code, the debtor proposes a repayment plan that lasts three to five years. In return for monthly repayments to creditors, the debtor is permitted to retain all property, even that which a trustee would liquidate under Chapter 7. After court confirmation of the plan, a private trustee receives the payments from the debtor and makes distribution to creditors. Historically, 30 percent of personal bankruptcies have been Chapter 13 cases.

Bankruptcy Petitions and Schedules

Debtors under all chapters of the Bankruptcy Code are required to file, under oath, a petition, schedules of assets and liabilities, and a statement of financial affairs. This initial paperwork is the key to identifying the debtor's assets, debts, and income. The bankruptcy system is self-reporting, like the internal revenue system. The debtor is expected to list assets, debts, and income accurately and completely on the petition and schedules.

For this study, we focused on Chapter 7 and Chapter 13 cases (individual, nonbusiness bankruptcies).

CHAPTER THREE

Effects of the Utilization of IRS Expense Standards on the Courts

One can attempt to assess the effects on the courts by reviewing the types and volume of issues ending up in the courts, the case law, and the administrative burden that implementing the new law has placed on the courts. In this chapter, we first review the case law and then review a report produced by the Administrative Office of the U.S. Courts (AO) regarding workload increases as a result of BAPCPA.

The major impacts flowing from use of the IRS standards as part of the means test are (1) increased litigation stemming from disputes regarding the appropriate application of the standards in particular circumstances and (2) due to divergent findings among the jurisdictions, uncertainty and nonuniform rules for similarly situated debtors in consumer bankruptcy cases. Participants in the qualitative interviews noted differing judicial opinions related to the new law and the confusion emanating from the differing opinions. According to the interview participants, judges across the country and even within the same district are interpreting the law differently.

In BAPCPA, Congress set out to reduce abuse of Chapter 7 by the minority of consumer debtors who have enough disposable income to make substantial repayment of unsecured debt. Such debtors would be barred from Chapter 7 protection but could still seek a discharge under Chapter 11 or Chapter 13, in which they would have to make payments to creditors over a term of years. To this end, Congress adopted the means test for each above-median–income debtor, estimating future repayment capacity using a six-month historical average for income and some expenses, plus incorporating IRS expense standards for the major items of food, clothing, transportation, and housing. Under Chapter 7, the test identifies presumed abusers, whose cases may be dismissed unless they voluntarily convert their cases to Chapter 13. Under Chapter 13, the means test, with a few adjustments, determines how much disposable income each above-median–income debtor must pay to general, unsecured creditors under the plan.

Under both chapters 11 and 13, the test is a method of estimating how much money the debtor is likely to have in the next five years, after payment of living expenses and secured and priority debt. It is too soon to tell whether it will provide more accurate estimates than prior methods have.

Computing Projected Disposable Income in Chapter 13

Whether the means test is now the only method for setting payments to unsecured creditors has been contested, especially under Chapter 13. Chapter 13 has long required debtors to make payments over three to five years. Courts formerly had considerable discretion to determine projected disposable income, especially regarding allowable expenditures. BAPCPA's revisions to Chapter 13 appear to formally limit that discretion, at least for above-median–income debtors. First, the Bankruptcy Code now directs that computation of disposable income begin with the means test's current monthly income. *Current monthly income* is an average of the debtor's income for the six months before filing, excluding Social Security income, child support, foster care, and disability payments for children. Next, the Bankruptcy Code says that disposable income for above-median–income, Chapter 13 debtors shall be computed using means test expenses, which include the IRS standards (11 USC §1325[b][2–3]). Participants in the qualitative interviews claimed that one of the BAPCPA's effects is the removal of judicial discretion for deciding on reasonable expenses. For instance, participants noted that judges can no longer rule against permitting someone with a large car loan to claim it as a reasonable offset against income and no longer have the discretion to use actual amounts spent on rent or mortgage; instead, they must use the IRS expense standards.

BAPCPA did not change the requirement for each debtor to file schedules I and J, which list actual income and expenses. Often, a debtor's expense allowance according to the IRS standard will differ from the debtor's actual current expenses reported on Schedule J (see Table 4.4 in Chapter Four). Actual income on Schedule I may also differ from the current monthly income's historical average. When there has been a significant change in the debtor's financial circumstances or the means-test results show less disposable income than schedules I minus J yield, Chapter 13 trustees may argue that the statutory term *projected disposable income* means something different from the term *disposable income* (not preceded by *projected*) computed using the means test. They may object to confirmation, contending that the court should depart from the means-test result and require the debtor to pay more into the plan, usually based on subtracting Schedule J expenses from Schedule I income. When actual income has greatly declined, debtors may argue that the means test is not the last word on required payments. Some courts have held that the statute's plain language gives them no discretion and that the projected disposable income to be paid to unsecured creditors is the same as the disposable income found by subtracting means-test expenses from current monthly income. (See, e.g., *In re Farrar-Johnson*, 353 B.R. 224, Bankr. N.D. Ill., September 15, 2006; *In re Alexander*, 344 B.R. 742, Bankr. E.D.N.C., August 23, 2006; and *In re Guzman*, 345 B.R. 640, Bankr. E.D. Wis., July 19, 2006.)

Many other courts, however, have found ways to depart from that formula, either by treating it merely as a starting point or by holding that disposable income is different from projected disposable income, which they then compute in a couple of ways. Some courts account for changes in financial circumstances when compared with the means-test calculations, while other courts follow the method used prior to BAPCPA, using Schedule I income less Schedule J expenses, perhaps disallowing some of the latter as unreasonable. (See, e.g., *In re Hardacre*,

338 B.R. 718, Bankr. N.D. Tex., March 6, 2006; *In re Fuller*, 346 B.R. 472, Bankr. S.D. Ill., June 21, 2006; and *In re Risher*, 344 B.R. 833, Bankr. W.D. Ky., July 12, 2006.)

Again, in our qualitative interviews, participants reported variations in the use of form B22C (Statement of Current Monthly Income and Calculation of Commitment Period and Disposable Income) vis-à-vis schedules I and J in calculating expenses. For example, in some regions, debtors are allowed to use the IRS expense standards (B22C) or the actual expenses listed in Schedule J, whichever is greater. Trustees in other regions focus on the income and expenses listed in schedules I and J when calculating disposable income rather than using form B22C and the IRS expense standards. Still other participants reported that, in their districts, only form B22C is used.

These differences of opinion have led to litigation, with the outcome that similarly situated debtors may have substantially different payment obligations depending on the jurisdiction in which they live. The differing burden of payment among the jurisdictions is likely to produce disparities in the relative proportions of Chapter 7 versus Chapter 13 filings as well as in rate of confirmation and completion of Chapter 13 plans among similarly situated debtors.

Interpretation of the IRS Expense Standards in Bankruptcy Courts

A number of questions of statutory interpretation of the IRS expense standards have been brought to the bankruptcy courts. On these, bankruptcy courts have frequently disagreed. BAPCPA took effect too recently for appellate courts to have had time to settle the many open questions. As a result, there is nonuniformity among federal judicial districts in application of the IRS expense standards under chapters 7 and 13. This chapter focuses on cases directly implicating the IRS standards in the means test. In particular, we review case law regarding the scope of Congress' adoption of the *Internal Revenue Manual*, the treatment of paid-off cars, allowances for ownership expense deduction for cars and homes that the debtor plans to surrender, and conflicts between IRS policies and important concerns in bankruptcy.

Adopting the IRS Expense Standards

To implement the means test, Congress adopted expense standards developed by the IRS for use in payment plans for delinquent taxpayers. These Collection Financial Standards include the national and local standards, as well as a list of other necessary expenses, and are set out in the *Internal Revenue Manual*.[1] The national standards set fixed dollar amounts, based on household size and income, to cover food, clothing, personal care, housekeeping supplies, and an allowance of $110 to $193 for miscellaneous expenses. The IRS allows taxpayers to deduct the national standard amount regardless of their actual expenses.

---

[1] The numbers in the Collection Financial Standards are drawn from a variety of sources. The national standards (for food and clothing) are derived from the Bureau of Labor Statistics (BLS) Consumer Expenditure Survey that the U.S. Census Bureau conducts annually. The IRS has established the miscellaneous allowance. The transportation ownership standards are based on new and used car financing data compiled by the Federal Reserve. Operating costs are derived from BLS data. Housing and utility standards are derived from U.S. Census Bureau and BLS data and are provided by state down to the county level. (See IRS, undated.)

The IRS treats the local standards differently, however, setting dollar figures for transportation and housing expenses that the IRS uses as caps on actual expenses. In other words, for transportation and housing, the taxpayer may deduct only his or her actual and reasonable expenses and is limited to the local standards even if actual expenses are greater (*Internal Revenue Manual*, p. 5.15.1.7). For categories called *Other Necessary Expenses*, the IRS allows the debtor to deduct actual and reasonable expenses in particular categories without a maximum limit, but the expenses must be necessary for income production or family health and welfare (*Internal Revenue Manual*, p. 5.15.1.7).

Many of the questions raised by importing these IRS expense standards into the bankruptcy arena stem from differences of opinion regarding congressional intent. Did Congress intend to adopt the IRS expense categories and dollar figures but to use bankruptcy law and policy to determine how to apply those standards in bankruptcy? Or did Congress intend bankruptcy courts to be bound by all the IRS's interpretations, usages, and extensions of those standards in the *Internal Revenue Manual*?

Section 707(b)(2)(A)(ii)(I) of the Bankruptcy Code directs use of the IRS standards for the means test as follows:

> The debtor's monthly expenses shall be the debtor's *applicable* monthly expense *amounts specified* under the National Standards and Local Standards, and the debtor's *actual* monthly *expenses* for the categories specified as Other Necessary Expenses issued by the Internal Revenue Service, . . . as in effect on the date of the order for relief. . . . (emphasis added)

Congress used the words "applicable . . . amounts specified" when referring to deductions under the national and local standards, in contrast to "actual . . . expenses" for other necessary expenses. Some courts see this difference in usage as authorizing debtors to use the standards as fixed-dollar deductions, even if the amounts specified exceed the debtors' actual expenses for housing and transportation. (See e.g., *In re Fowler*, 349 B.R. 414, 417–418, Bankr. D. Del., September 11, 2006; and *In re Demonica*, 345 B.R. 895, 902, Bankr. N.D. Ill., July 31, 2006.) For the other necessary expense categories, on the other hand, the Bankruptcy Code's text clearly limits deductions to actual expenses. However, other courts suggest that Congress intended to adopt IRS usage as well as dollar amounts and decline to follow *In re Fowler* and *In re Demonica*. (See e.g., *In re Slusher*, 2007 WL 118009, Bankr. D. Nev., January 17, 2007; and *In re McGuire*, 342 B.R. 608, 613, Bankr. W.D. Mo., June 1, 2006.)

In the Chapter 7 context, at least, using fixed-dollar allowances for some major categories makes the means test easy to apply. Further, the means test may not be the last word on abuse. Even if the presumption of abuse arises, the debtor can rebut this presumption by establishing special circumstances that justify an adjustment to his or her income and expenses that reduces MDI to below the presumptively abusive level. Further, if the presumption of abuse does not arise, in part because the IRS standards exceed a particular debtor's actual expenses, section 707(b)(3) allows dismissal of the case if the totality of the debtor's financial circumstances indicates abuse.

Treatment of Paid-Off Cars

The proper treatment of paid-off cars is unsettled. The IRS transportation allowance has two parts: first, an allowance for operating expenses of up to two cars or public transport if the debtor does not own or lease a vehicle; and second, an ownership allowance for purchase or lease costs for up to two cars. Debtors in bankruptcy often own older-model cars on which no loans are outstanding at time of filing. May the debtor take an auto ownership deduction for that car in the means test?

USTP has urged bankruptcy courts to deny an ownership allowance on these facts, contending that the deduction is not applicable under section 707(b)(2), since the IRS would deny the allowance on a paid-off car. In effect, some courts and USTP read "applicable monthly expense amounts" to import not only the dollar amounts and expense categories, but also IRS practice as set forth in the *Internal Revenue Manual*. When debtors attempt to justify the deduction because they will soon need to replace an older, paid-off car, the response is that a Chapter 13 plan can be modified if and when that need arises. A number of cases adopt this position and disallow the ownership deduction. (See *In re McGuire*, 342 B.R. 608, 613, Bankr. W.D. Mo., June 1, 2006; *In re Hardacre*, 338 B.R. 718, 728, Bankr. N.D. Tex., March 6, 2006; and *In re Wiggs*, 2006 WL 2246432, Bankr. N.D. Ill., August 4, 2006.)

Other courts disagree and would accord a more limited effect to "applicable amounts specified." They take the position that, while Congress adopted the IRS's "amounts specified," BAPCPA's means test functions so differently from the IRS's individually negotiated payment plans that Congress did not intend to import all IRS usage into the means test. These courts allow the full deduction for cars that the debtor owns even if the car is paid off, in reliance on the statutory text and legislative history. (See e.g., *In re Fowler*, 349 B.R. 414, 417–418, Bankr. D. Del., September 11, 2006; *In re Demonica*, 345 B.R. 895, 903–905, Bankr. N.D. Ill., July 31, 2006; *In re Wilson*, 356 B.R. 114, Bankr. D. Del., December 11, 2006; *In re Hartwick*, 352 B.R. 867, Bankr. D. Minn., October 13, 2006; and *In re Haley*, 354 B.R. 340, Bankr. D.N.H., October 18, 2006 [debtor may take means-test ownership deduction for car even if debtor has no ongoing car payment].)

Recently, the IRS addresses the older-car situation by allowing delinquent taxpayers an additional deduction of $200 per month if they own a car more than six years old or with more than 75,000 miles on the odometer. This "tired-iron" deduction is not part of the national or local standards or other necessary expenses that Congress adopted in section 707(b)(2). However, some courts and USTP suggest that this IRS practice should now be followed in bankruptcy to compute the means-test deduction for paid-off cars. (See, e.g., *In re Slusher*, 2007 WL 118009, Bankr. D. Nev., January 17, 2007; and *In re Barraza*, 346 B.R. 724, Bankr. N.D. Tex. 2006.)

Ownership Expense Deduction for Cars and Homes That the Debtor Plans to Surrender

Another question dividing the courts is whether a debtor may take an ownership expense deduction for cars and homes that the debtor plans to surrender in the course of the case. Some courts deny any ownership deduction in such a case. Others direct the debtor to compute means-test deductions as of the filing date. So long as the debtor still owns the asset at that point, he or she gets the full ownership expense deduction. Still other courts adopt an intermediate view, permitting or denying the ownership deduction depending on whether and how soon the debtor plans to purchase or lease a replacement car or home. Similar questions arise with the non-IRS deduction for secured debt under the means test. (See *In re Walker*, 2006 WL 1314125, Bankr. N.D. Ga., May 1, 2006; *In re Oliver*, 2006 WL 2086691, Bankr. D. Or., June 29, 2006 [debtors may deduct secured-debt payments even though they will surrender the collateral]; and *In re Ray*, 2007 WL 690131, Bankr. D.S.C., February 28, 2007 [debtors may not take secured-debt deductions for collateral they intend to surrender].)

IRS Policies That Conflict with Important Bankruptcy Concerns

Sometimes, IRS policies run directly counter to other concerns in bankruptcy. The IRS allows a deduction for other necessary expenses only if the taxpayer proves that the expenses are "necessary . . . for . . . a taxpayer's . . . health and welfare and/or production of income" (*Internal Revenue Manual*, p. 5.15.1.7). In a recent case, the court disallowed $100 per month in charitable contributions that an above-median–income, Chapter 13 debtor proposed to deduct when computing disposable income. The court denied the deduction because the debtor had failed to show that the contributions were necessary for health or income production (*In re Diagostino*, 347 B.R. 116, Bankr. N.D.N.Y., August 28, 2006; see also *In re Meyer*, 355 B.R. 837, Bankr. D.N.M., December 4, 2006; and *In re Tranmer*, 355 B.R. 234, Bankr. D. Mont., November 16, 2006 [charitable contributions not allowed for above-median–income, Chapter 13 debtors]). The *Diagostino* decision was criticized as contrary to the bankruptcy policy of permitting continued charitable contributions. Within six months, Congress overturned that result and affirmed debtors' right to deduct tithes and other charitable contributions in Chapter 13. (See Public Law 109-439, 2006.)

Although Congress has amended the Bankruptcy Code to protect charitable contributions under Chapter 13, the question remains whether other necessary expense deductions under Chapter 7 or for purposes other than contributions must meet the IRS's necessity standards. For cases holding that debtors in bankruptcy must make such a showing for other necessary expense deductions, see, e.g., *Baxter v. Johnson* (346 B.R. 256, Bankr. S.D. Ga., July 21, 2006) and *In re Lara* (347 B.R. 198, Bankr. N.D. Tex., June 28, 2006).

Thus, interpretation of the IRS standards has proven controversial, and many questions remain unsettled. Because these questions concern the grant or denial of deductions, IRS standards' effects on debtors may vary among the jurisdictions. For example, a jurisdiction that denies an ownership deduction for paid-off cars may bar many more debtors from Chapter 7 protection than may one that allows that deduction. Whether unsecured creditors can, in fact, collect more from debtors denied the deduction, either outside of bankruptcy or under Chapter 13, however, is a question for later empirical investigation.

Workload on the Courts

Congress asked the AO to report on BAPCPA's impact on the federal judiciary. The AO delivered its report to Congress in August 2006 (AO, 2006). The AO found that BAPCPA implementation has resulted in a substantial amount of new work for bankruptcy courts, especially for clerks and administrators.

The report indicates that the effects on judges seem to vary greatly depending upon the district. Most judges seem to agree that each case now requires more of their time. This is not surprising, given the fact that BAPCPA created more than 35 new types of motions, objections, and hearings that did not previously exist. For new provisions of the law, judges must analyze each new issue or question, make a decision, and then report the decision to the bar through written opinions, orders, or instructions. Some judges report a heavier load due to the new provisions, while other judges say that they have yet to see many new problems created through BAPCPA. The report states that many of the judges suspect that, as the number of filings creep up, the overall workload will also increase.

The AO report does not attribute an increase in workload to a particular provision of the new law; therefore, what portion may be due to the IRS expense standards is not known. We did probe this issue during our interviews and group discussions, and we gleaned some contextual information from those discussions. There was mixed opinion among participants as to whether BAPCPA has brought changes in the number of motions filed. Some participants reported that the number of motions filed in their districts has decreased because there has been a drop in the number of bankruptcy cases since BAPCPA was enacted. Other participants reported that, despite the drop in bankruptcy cases, there has been an increase in the number of motions filed in their districts since the law was passed. However, few believed that this increase in motions is related to the IRS expense standards. Instead, they noted that there have been more hearings about how sections of the law regarding the use of the standards should be interpreted. Those participants who did attribute the increase in motions to the IRS expense standards reported that, in their districts, there have been many hearings over vehicle-related expenses.

CHAPTER FOUR

Empirical Analyses of the Effects of IRS Expense Standard Use on Debtors

We drew samples of cases that had been filed in eight bankruptcy court districts that are representative of bankruptcy filings across the country. For each district, we calculated the fraction of Chapter 7 and Chapter 13 cases, respectively, by debtors with above-median incomes who therefore were required to use the IRS expense standards in calculating their MDIs. For above-median–income, Chapter 13 debtors, we calculated what their MDIs would have been had they used their reported current expenses instead of the IRS standards and compared the results. These comparisons demonstrate the extent to which the use of the IRS standards affected debtors' MDIs. We explored the relationships between the differences in the two calculations of MDIs and debtors' financial circumstances to examine the extent to which some types of debtors, distinguished by their financial circumstances or the district in which they filed, are more or less affected by use of the IRS standards. The details of each of these steps in the analysis are discussed below.

Bankruptcy Case Samples

To support empirical analyses of the effects of using the IRS expense standards, we drew samples of cases filed in a representative set of bankruptcy court districts across the country. We consulted with EOUST to select a set of districts in which filings are generally representative of bankruptcy filings across the country. We selected the eight districts listed in Table 1.1 in Chapter One.

Bankruptcy filings are often not perfectly correct. Debtors fill out the forms and schedules in varying levels of detail. In some cases, we noted an exacting level of detail in documenting expenses (some itemizing the number and price of haircuts), while others used very broad categories. In other cases, we noted debtors' frequent failure to amend the summary of schedules when amendments were filed for other schedules. We corrected this inconsistency by adjusting the summary of schedules with the updated information from the amendments. We used the summary of schedules data to capture the sample's overall characteristics. Moreover, both our review of case law and our interviews suggest that the IRS standards are not uniformly applied either within or across districts. We had no basis for adjusting these inconsistencies and had to accept the cases as they were filed.

Individual bankruptcy filings surged in September and October 2005 in anticipation of BAPCPA's effective date. Presumably, a large number of individuals considering bankruptcy decided that they would fare better under the then-existing law than under the law as modified by BAPCPA. This raises the possibility that the pool of debtors filing for bankruptcy in the months immediately following BAPCPA's effective date might include a disproportionate number of debtors whose cases were not sensitive to the revisions introduced by BAPCPA. We thought that it might take some months before the pool of debtors filing for bankruptcy reflected the long-term, typical pool. We also thought that it might take some months for debtors and their advisors to become sufficiently familiar with BAPCPA that their cases reflected the effects of BAPCPA's provisions.

We wished to draw cases that had been filed sufficiently long after BAPCPA took effect that they would likely reflect both the typical pool of debtors filing for bankruptcy and the effects of BAPCPA. However, a sizable fraction of cases are withdrawn, significantly modified, converted (from a Chapter 7 to a Chapter 13 case or conversely), or dismissed after they are filed. These changes are frequently caused by the discovery of errors in the original filing or by trustees' or bankruptcy court judges' decisions regarding the case's appropriate disposition. In these instances, some of the information that the debtor originally provided might have been erroneous. Accordingly, we thought it important to draw cases that had been filed sufficiently long before we drew them that we could reasonably expect that USTP analysts and trustees had reviewed the information that the debtor provided and not found any egregious error.

In consultation with EOUST, we decided that April 1, 2006, was a date sufficiently long after BAPCPA took effect that cases filed on or after that date were likely to reflect the effects of BAPCPA on the typical pool of debtors going through bankruptcy. Also, USTP and the Chapter 13 trustee would likely have completed their reviews of the case by the time we began to draw the samples in November 2006.

We drew the first 50 Chapter 7 cases filed in each of the selected districts on or immediately after April 1, 2006, in the order in which they were filed, that had not been dismissed or converted to a Chapter 13 case by December 8, 2006. We also drew the first 100 Chapter 13 cases filed by an above-median–income debtor in each of the selected districts on or after April 1, 2006, that had not been dismissed or converted to a Chapter 7 case by December 8, 2006. Because Chapter 13 cases typically result in a repayment plan that extends three to five years, we could not limit the sample to cases discharged by a date within this study's time frame. We drew cases filed voluntarily only by individuals, whether filing individually or jointly. We did not include filings by entities other than individuals.

While drawing these samples of Chapter 13 cases, we counted the Chapter 13 cases in which the debtor's income was below the applicable median. This allowed us to calculate the fraction of Chapter 13 cases in which the debtor was not required to use the IRS expense standards.

We did not include dismissed or converted cases. Cases generally are dismissed or converted because staff in the U.S. trustee's office or the trustee to whom the case was assigned discover that the debtor's financial condition did not satisfy the criteria for a particular filing. This may reflect a misunderstanding by the debtor as to the criteria or a deliberate or inadvertent misstatement regarding some aspect of the debtor's financial condition. Dismissals or conversions might also reflect the debtor changing his or her mind (say, because a creditor is willing to negotiate with him or her after filing or because the trustee takes an interest in property that is arguably exempt and the debtor decides to convert rather than litigate against the trustee's decision). In any event, we have no way of knowing whether debtors whose Chapter 7 filings were dismissed or converted were affected by the use of the IRS standards, so we excluded them from the sample.

When we combined the cases from all eight sample districts to obtain an estimate for all districts, we weighted the result for each individual district by the total number of filings under the relevant chapter in that district between April 1 and September 30, 2006. These weights reflect the number of filings that each selected filing represents. Thus, a result for all districts with respect to some aspect of Chapter 7 or 13 filing reflects the distribution of chapter 7 and 13 filings across the eight districts during this six-month period. By weighting the results, the estimates presented here are representative of all the filings in these eight districts and thus one-sixth of the bankruptcy filings in the country. Because the districts included in our samples were selected to be representative of districts across the country, our results for all districts should be representative of bankruptcy cases, on average, across the country.

Fraction of Chapter 7 Cases Using the IRS Standards

Debtors who file under Chapter 7 are not affected by the use of the IRS expense standards if their incomes are below median. Above-median–income debtors, on the other hand, may file under Chapter 7 only if their MDIs, calculated using the IRS expense standards for certain expense categories, fall below a specified threshold. Specifically, an above-median–income debtor is presumed to be filing abusively under Chapter 7 if his or her 60-month disposable income, calculated using the IRS expense standards, is greater than $10,000 or, if less than $10,000 and greater than $6,000, is more than 25 percent of his or her nonpriority, unsecured debt. Accordingly, the use of the IRS expense standards to calculate MDI can affect whether above-median–income debtors will be allowed to file under Chapter 7.

We can observe the fraction of above-median–income debtors whose total deductions, including the IRS expense standards, resulted in an MDI below the abuse threshold. We cannot observe the number of above-median–income debtors who wished to file under Chapter 7 but were precluded from doing so because the use of the IRS standards resulted in MDIs higher than the means test allows. Accordingly, we cannot empirically estimate the extent to which the use of the IRS standards affected would-be Chapter 7 filers. We can observe only the fraction of Chapter 7 cases filed by above-median–income debtors.

Table 4.1 presents the fraction of the 50 Chapter 7 cases we drew in each district filed by an above-median–income debtor. The estimate for all districts is the weighted fraction of all Chapter 7 cases in the eight samples. It also shows the 95-percent confidence interval for each estimate.[1]

[1] The 95-percent confidence interval is the range within which, if the sampling were repeated numerous times, the estimate would fall 95 percent of the time.

Table 4.1
Chapter 7 Cases Using the IRS Standards

Judicial District	Chapter 7 Cases Using IRS Standards (%)	95-Percent Confidence Interval (%)	
		Low	High
E.D.N.Y.	14	4.4	23.6
W.D. Tex.	24	12.2	35.8
W.D. Tenn.	16	5.8	26.2
N.D. Ohio	2	0	5.9
S.D. Iowa	6	0	12.6
C.D. Cal.	0	0	0
D. Utah	4	0	9.4
M.D. Fla.	10	1.7	18.3
All districts	7	4.5	9.1

Overall, about 7 percent of the sample Chapter 7 debtors had above-median incomes but could file under Chapter 7 because their expense deductions allowed them to calculate MDIs that escaped the presumption.

There was noticeable variation across judicial districts in the fraction of Chapter 7 filers who had above-median incomes. Our sample of debtors who filed for Chapter 7 protection in the Central District of California did not include a single above-median–income debtor; thus no Chapter 7 case in our sample from the Central District of California used the IRS expense standards to meet the criteria for a Chapter 7 filing. In three other districts, the Northern District of Ohio, Southern District of Iowa, and District of Utah, fewer than 6 percent of Chapter 7 filers had above-median incomes and used the IRS standards to file under Chapter 7.

However, in four districts, the Eastern District of New York, Western District of Texas, Western District of Tennessee, and Middle District of Florida, 10 percent or more of the debtors who filed under Chapter 7 had above-median incomes but deductions, including those based on IRS standards, that resulted in MDIs below the abuse threshold.

The fraction of Chapter 7 cases filed by above-median–income debtors varies considerably among the sample districts. In some districts, e.g., in the Central District of California, above-median–income debtors either file under Chapter 13 or do not file at all. But, in other districts, e.g., in the Western District of Texas, a substantial number of above-median–income debtors apparently satisfy the means test and file under Chapter 7. In brief, the effects of the means test, including the use of the IRS standards, on would-be Chapter 7 filers are very uneven: substantial in some parts of the country and inconsequential in others.

Again, our data reflect only the number of above-median–income debtors whose MDIs, computed using the IRS standards, escaped the presumption for filing under Chapter 7. We cannot observe above-median–income debtors who wished to file under Chapter 7 but did not do so because use of the IRS standards resulted in MDI figures too high to escape the presumption. Similarly, we have no way to determine how many above-median–income debtors who did not file under Chapter 7 because their MDIs, calculated using IRS standards, were too high would have escaped the presumption had they been allowed to use their current expenses to calculate their MDIs. Consequently, we cannot estimate the effects of the use of the IRS standards in calculating a debtor's deductions on above-median–income debtors who considered filing under Chapter 7.

Fraction of Chapter 13 Cases Using the IRS Standards

As noted previously, we drew the first 100 Chapter 13 cases filed by above-median–income debtors in each of the selected districts on or after April 1, 2006, that had not been dismissed or converted to a Chapter 7 case by December 8, 2006. While drawing these samples of Chapter 13 cases, we counted the Chapter 13 cases filed by below-median–income debtors. This allowed us to estimate the fraction of Chapter 13 cases filed by above-median–income debtors. Only above-median–income debtors use the IRS expense standards.

Table 4.2 presents the number of Chapter 13 cases we drew in each sample district in which the debtor's income was above median, requiring that the IRS standards be used. The estimate of the percent using IRS standards in all districts is the weighted average of the results for the individual districts. The weight for each district is the number of Chapter 13 filings in that district between April 1 and September 30, 2006.

Overall, slightly more than one-quarter of the Chapter 13 filers in our samples had above-median incomes and, consequently, were required to use the IRS expense standards to calculate their MDIs. Almost three-quarters of the debtors who filed under Chapter 13 had below-median incomes. These debtors, and possibly some of those with above-median incomes, presumably could have filed under Chapter 7 had they so chosen but opted for Chapter 13

Table 4.2
Chapter 13 Cases Using the IRS Standards

Judicial District	Chapter 13 Cases		Cases Using IRS Standards (Above-Median Income) (%)	95-Percent Confidence Interval (%)	
	Above Median	Below Median		Low	High
E.D.N.Y.	100	51	66	59	74
W.D. Tex.	100	172	37	31	43
W.D. Tenn.	100	675	13	10	15
N.D. Ohio	100	262	28	23	32
S.D. Iowa	100	132	43	37	50
C.D. Cal.	100	93	52	45	59
D. Utah	100	223	31	26	36
M.D. Fla.	100	195	34	28	39
All districts	800	1,803	27	25	29

instead. During our interviews, we were told that some debtors who were eligible for Chapter 7 protection nevertheless chose to file under Chapter 13. One reason for this choice is to cover the attorney's fees when the debtor did not have enough money to pay the fees up front. Many participants in both the focus group and interviews commented on the fact that filing fees and attorney's fees have gone up since BAPCPA's enactment. Attorney's fees for a Chapter 7 filing are typically paid up front, before the bankruptcy. Chapter 13 attorney's fees are often rolled into the payment plan for all creditors, and some judicial districts require that such fees be part of the plan and paid over time rather than being paid in one lump sum.

Another reason that below-median–income debtors may choose to file under Chapter 13 even when eligible for Chapter 7 protection is that they are behind on the payments for their cars or mortgages and wish to stop foreclosure and cure the default by spreading the arrears over the life of the plan. Chapter 7 does not provide a right to cure defaults. Some debtors may also prefer Chapter 13 because it provides a broader discharge than does Chapter 7.

There was substantial variation across judicial districts in the fraction of Chapter 13 filers whose income exceeded the median and, consequently, had to use the IRS expense standards to calculate their MDIs. The proportion of such above-median–income debtors filing under Chapter 13 was similar to the corresponding national average in only three judicial districts: the Northern District of Ohio, District of Utah, and Middle District of Florida.

The proportion of above-median–income debtors filing under Chapter 13 in the Eastern District of New York, the Western District of Texas, the Southern District of Iowa, and the Central District of California was well above the average for all sample districts. The lower bound of the 95-percent confidence interval in each of these cases was greater than was the upper bound of the 95-percent confidence interval for the national average.

Only 13 percent of the Chapter 13 debtors in the Western District of Tennessee had above-median incomes and, consequently, used the IRS expense standards in calculating their MDIs. Presumably, all the below-median–income debtors (about seven-eighths of the debtors who filed under Chapter 13) and some of those above the median in this judicial district could have filed under Chapter 7 but chose not to do so. The qualitative interviews revealed that this district has an historical culture of using Chapter 13 rather than Chapter 7 even by debtors with low incomes.

Here, too, it must be noted that our data reflect the extent to which debtors who filed under Chapter 13 used the IRS expense standards to compute their MDIs. We cannot observe above-median–income debtors who wished to file under Chapter 13, used the IRS standards to compute their MDIs as some districts require, and, because they thought that MDI would not give them enough flexibility to have a functional plan, did not file. Consequently, we have no data on the extent to which the IRS standards deterred would-be Chapter 13 filers.

Discussion of Using IRS Expense Allowances to Calculate MDI

BAPCPA requires above-median–income debtors to use the IRS expense standards rather than their current expenses for five categories of expenses to calculate their MDIs:

- living expenses (e.g., food, clothing, personal care, household supplies, miscellaneous)
- nonmortgage housing and utility expenses (e.g., utilities, repairs, maintenance)
- mortgage or rental expenses
- vehicle operation and public transportation expenses
- transportation ownership and lease expenses.

The allowance for living expenses varies with the debtor's income and family size, irrespective of where the debtor lives. The allowances for nonmortgage housing and utility expenses and for mortgage or rental expenses depend on the debtor's family size and county of residence. The vehicle operation and public transportation expense allowance depends on whether the debtor owns zero, one, or two cars and varies by SMSA or census region. The transportation ownership and lease expense allowance depends on whether the debtor has a loan or lease payment obligation on one or two cars. The amounts allowed are national figures.

Since BAPCPA took effect, debtors filing under Chapter 13 are required to complete form B22C.[2] If the debtor's income is above the applicable median, form B22C requires that the debtor calculate his or her MDI according to Bankruptcy Code specifications using the IRS standards for the aforementioned five expense categories. Accordingly, the form B22C filed by an above-median–income debtor lists the deductions that he or she took in the relevant IRS expense categories.

All debtors filing for bankruptcy report their current expenses on Schedule J. Accordingly, we can use the Schedule J information from each of our sample of above-median–income, Chapter 13 cases to identify each debtor's current expenses corresponding to each of the IRS expense categories.

Table 4.3 shows the lines on form B22C that list amounts that each debtor deducted when calculating his or her deductions using the IRS standards. It also shows the corresponding Schedule J current expense categories and the lines on which each debtor reported current expenses in each of the categories.

The allowance for living expenses, for nonmortgage housing and utility expenses, and for vehicle operation and public transportation expenses are straightforward. In each case, the debtor is allowed an IRS-specified amount, given his or her status. For example, the allowance for living expenses depends on the debtor's household size and income. In our interviews, some noted that this provision seemed unfair, since higher-income debtors are allowed to deduct more for food than are lower-income debtors.

The allowance for mortgage or rental expenses is similarly straightforward for renters. The debtor is allowed an amount specified by the IRS, the local standard for housing and utilities, which depends on the debtor's family size and county of residence.

The allowance for mortgage or rental expenses is more complex for homeowners. The debtor is allowed the IRS local standard for housing and utilities minus the debtor's average

[2] Above-median–income debtors who wish to file under Chapter 7 use form B22A (Statement of Current Monthly Income and Means Test Calculation) to determine whether they pass the means test. Above-median–income debtors filing under Chapter 13 use form B22C to calculate their MDIs. During 2006, the B was dropped from both form B22s. The B indicated that this was an interim form. That form ultimately was approved and is now referred to as Official Form 22. However, throughout this report, the form will be referred to as the B22.

Table 4.3
Correspondence Between Deductions Using IRS Standards and Those Using Schedule J Expenses

Deductions Using IRS Standards	B22C Line	Current Expense Category	Schedule J Line
Living expenses (e.g., food, clothing, personal care, household supplies, miscellaneous)	24	Food	4
		Clothing	5
		Laundry	6
		Recreation	9
Nonmortgage housing and utility expenses (e.g., utilities, repairs, maintenance)	25A	Utilities	2a, 2b, 2c, 2d
		Maintenance	3
Mortgage or rental expenses, renters	25B	Rent	1
		Homeowner's insurance	11a
		Property taxes	12
Mortgage or rental expenses, owners	25B	Homeowner's insurance	11a
		Property taxes	12
Vehicle operation and public transportation expenses	27	Transportation	8
		Auto insurance	11d
Transportation ownership and lease expenses (vehicle 1)	28	No corresponding current expense	
Transportation ownership and lease expenses (vehicle 2)	29	No corresponding current expense	

monthly payment for debts secured by his or her home if the difference is greater than zero. Mortgage debts include payments of taxes and insurance required by the mortgage. The allowance is zero if the IRS standard is less than the average monthly payment. For a homeowner who has paid off his or her home, the allowance equals the IRS standard. So, the IRS standards essentially allow homeowners a deduction equal to the difference, if greater than zero, between the IRS local standard for housing and utilities and the debtor's payment on debts secured by his or her home.

Debtors later (form B22C, line 47) deduct payments on secured claims, including home mortgage payments. Because homeowners are allowed to deduct the full amount of their payments on debts secured by their homes irrespective of the size of these payments relative to any IRS standard, they are allowed to deduct their mortgage payments in calculating their MDIs, which equals the deduction they would take if they were using their current expenses to compute their MDIs. There is no current expense corresponding to any additional deduction resulting from a mortgage payment that is less than the IRS local standard for housing and utilities (mortgage or rental expenses).

The IRS allowance for transportation ownership and lease expenses works similarly to the allowance for mortgage or rental expenses. A car owner is allowed to deduct the difference, if positive, between the IRS local standard for transportation ownership and lease expenses for vehicle 1 and his or her average monthly payment for debts secured by that vehicle. If the debtor owns a second car, he or she may deduct the difference, if positive, between the IRS local standard for transportation ownership and lease expenses for vehicle 2 and his or her average monthly payment for debts secured by that vehicle. In some districts, a vehicle owner who has paid off his or her first (or, in the case of vehicle 2, second) car is allowed to deduct the respective IRS local standard. Debtors later (on line 47) deduct payments on secured claims, which include payments on claims secured by their cars. Car owners are allowed to deduct the amount of their payments on debts secured by their cars irrespective of the size of these payments relative to any IRS standard. Debtors who lease one or two vehicles may deduct the IRS car ownership allowance for each car even if their lease payments are more than the IRS car ownership allowance.

BAPCPA changed the way in which a debtor filing under Chapter 13 treats vehicle ownership costs. Prior to BAPCPA, a Chapter 13 debtor typically did not deduct installment payments on a vehicle in calculating monthly net income. Schedule J instructs the debtor (line 13), "Installment Payments: (in Chapter 11, 12, and 13 cases, do not list payments to be included in the plan)." Because these payments would typically be included in the repayment plan, there is no current expense corresponding to the transportation ownership and lease expense allowance.

Again, these calculations apply to above-median–income debtors only. Below-median–income debtors who file under Chapter 13 do not use the IRS standards in calculating their MDIs.

Comparing the Use of IRS Standards with Use of Actual Expenses in Calculating MDI

We used the corresponding variables between the IRS standards and debtors' current expenses presented in Table 4.3 to examine how using the IRS expense standards to calculate MDI affected each debtor in our Chapter 13 samples. In the course of this analysis, we discovered that 27 of the sample cases had not completed one or more of the calculations specified by the Bankruptcy Code. Accordingly, we omitted these cases in the subsequent analyses.

Because a debtor's MDI equals his or her income minus his or her deductions, the difference between a debtor's MDI using the IRS standards and what his or her MDI would have been had the debtor used current expenses instead equals the difference between the deductions allowed using the IRS standards and the deductions the debtor would have been allowed had he or she instead used current expenses.

During the qualitative interviews and group discussions, we heard a variety of opinions regarding whether the IRS expense standards accurately reflected costs of living. Many participants indicated that the IRS expense standards were generous and that debtors were allowed higher expenses under BAPCPA than they would have been allowed previously. However, some interview participants indicated that the adequacy of the IRS expense standards varied on a case-by-case basis and, for some debtors, they were not adequate.

Opinions on the adequacy of the IRS mortgage or rental allowance seemed to reflect geographic or urban or rural differences. The majority of interview participants considered the mortgage or rental allowance adequate for rural areas but too low for urban areas, where real estate is usually more expensive.

We took each sample debtor's deductions calculated according to the Bankruptcy Code's specifications using IRS standards from form B22C. We then calculated the deductions that the debtor would have been allowed in the corresponding current expenses. Table 4.3 lists those deductions that use IRS standards and the corresponding current expenses. The result is what the debtor's deductions would have been had he or she used current expenses to calculate deductions rather than using the IRS standards. Debtors are allowed a variety of deductions for their expenses in categories other than those listed in Table 4.3. Deductions in expense categories other than those listed in Table 4.3 reflect the debtor's current expenses and are not based on any calculation using IRS standards. For example, debtors are allowed to deduct their taxes, other than real estate and sales taxes, such as income taxes, self-employment taxes, social security taxes, and Medicare taxes. Because deductions in categories other than those listed in Table 4.3 are not affected by the use of IRS standards, they are not considered in any of the results presented subsequently.

Table 4.4 presents the results for each of the eight districts and for all districts combined. It presents the number of cases for which we had complete information and the average debtors' IRS-related deductions (deductions calculated according the Bankruptcy Code specifications and using the IRS standards) and the average debtor's deductions using the corresponding current expenses.

The average debtor's IRS-related deductions are considerably higher than his or her corresponding deductions using current expenses in every district and in all districts combined.

Table 4.4 also shows, for each district and for all districts combined, the average difference between the IRS-related deductions and what the deductions would have been if they had used their current expenses instead. For example, the debtors in our Central District of California sample reported the highest IRS-related deductions, on average, of all the districts in which we drew samples of cases. Their average deductions using the IRS standards were $3,253. Their average corresponding current expenses were $2,712. On average, when debtors in the Central District of California used the IRS standards in calculating their deductions, they were allowed to deduct $542 more than if they had used their current expenses instead.[3]

The use of IRS standards rather than current expenses to calculate a debtor's deductions results in greater deductions and, consequently, a lower MDI, on average, in each sample district and in all districts combined. On average, debtors' deductions are $490 greater in all districts combined when the IRS standards are used than if current expenses had been used instead. In individual districts, the average increases in deductions due to the use of the IRS standards ranges from $311 in the Middle District of Florida to $612 in the Northern District of Ohio. The IRS standards result in larger deductions, on average, yielding lower MDIs across the country.

[3] Table 4.4 also shows the probability, p, that, given the observed variation in the data, the result could have occurred by chance. The odds that an estimate for which $p < 0.001$ occurred by chance are less than one in 1,000.

Table 4.4
Difference in Deductions Calculated Using IRS Standards and Those Using Corresponding Current Expenses

		Average IRS-Related Deductions ($)		Deductions Using IRS Standards Minus Deductions Using Current Expenses ($)				
					Percentile			
Judicial District	N	Using IRS Standards	Current Expenses	Average[a]	75th	50th	25th	Percent Negative[b]
E.D.N.Y.	96	2,941	2,343	598	983	624	196	20
W.D. Tex.	100	2,326	1,888	437	806	440	130	15
W.D. Tenn.	93	2,154	1,728	426	784	498	106	19
N.D. Ohio	96	2,500	1,887	612	941	569	268	9
S.D. Iowa	99	2,439	2,036	402	729	331	55	19
C.D. Cal.	97	3,253	2,712	542	1,174	696	122	21
D. Utah	98	2,589	2,004	585	975	578	270	14
M.D. Fla.	94	2,372	2,061	311	652	306	57	19
All districts	773	2,572	2,083	490	859	496	150	17

[a] $p < 0.001$ on standard t-test and $p < 0.05$ on sign and sign-rank tests for every district and for all districts.

[b] These indicate the percent of sample cases for which the current expenses yielded a greater deduction than did the IRS standards, resulting in a negative number when calculating the difference.

We used standard t-tests to estimate the probability that the average differences between the deductions allowed using IRS standards and the deductions that would have been allowed using current expenses were each significantly different from zero. Because there were clear outliers in the data, we were not confident in the significance level indicated by the t-tests. Accordingly, we also ran nonparametric sign and sign-rank tests. The average difference between deductions calculated using the IRS standards and those using their corresponding current expenses was significantly different from zero on both the t-tests and the nonparametric tests for all districts combined and for each of the individual districts.

Table 4.4 also shows the 75th, 50th (median), and 25th percentiles in the distribution of differences between the deductions allowed using the IRS standards and the deductions that would have been allowed had current expenses been used instead. Because the IRS standards allow greater deductions in almost all sample cases, the difference between the two is positive in the large majority of cases in every district. But the IRS standards do not yield greater deductions in every case. Accordingly, Table 4.4 also shows the percent of cases in each district in which the difference between the two calculations is negative. In these cases, the deductions allowed using the IRS standards are less than the deductions based on the corresponding current expenses.

For example, 75 percent of the debtors in our sample from the Southern District of Iowa were allowed IRS-related deductions that exceeded their corresponding current expenses by $729 or less. For these debtors, their MDIs, calculated using the IRS standards, was no more than $729 less than what their MDI would have been had they used their current expenses in the calculation. In other words, 25 percent of the debtors in this sample had an MDI that was reduced by at least $729 below what it would have been if current expenses had been used to calculate their deductions.

The median, or 50th-percentile, debtor is the debtor whose difference falls in the center of the distribution among the debtors in his or her district; half of the debtors in his or her district had larger differences and half had smaller differences. The 25th-percentile debtor is the debtor whose difference is less than 75 percent of the debtors in his or her district or in all districts combined. For example, for half of the debtors in our Southern District of Iowa sample, the difference between their deductions using the IRS standards and what their deductions would have been had they used their current expenses was at least $331. And, for half the debtors in that sample, the difference between their deductions using the IRS standards and what their deductions would have been had they used their current expenses was less than $331. Similarly, one-quarter of the debtors in our Southern District of Iowa sample had IRS-related deductions that exceed their current expense–based deductions by $55 or less.

The 25th, 50th, and 75th percentiles in the rankings of the differences between debtors' deductions calculated using either the IRS standards or the debtors' current expenses are greater than zero in every district. At least three-quarters of the sample Chapter 13 cases in each district had greater IRS-related deductions than their corresponding current expenses, so their deductions, calculated using the IRS standards, are larger than what their deductions would have been had they used their current expenses to do the calculation.

However, for some debtors in each district, use of the IRS standards resulted in lower deductions than if they had used current expenses instead. For these debtors, the difference between the two calculations is negative. The percent of such debtors ranges from 9 percent in the Northern District of Ohio to 21 percent in the Central District of California.

Effects of Using Specific IRS Standards

As noted in Table 4.3, the IRS expense standards apply to five expense categories: living expenses, nonmortgage housing and utility expenses, mortgage or rental housing expenses, vehicle operation and public transportation expenses, and transportation ownership and lease expenses for the debtor's first and second cars. To explore the effects of each of these categories on debtors, we calculated the differences between the deductions allowed under the calculations specified by the Bankruptcy Code using the IRS standard and debtors' current expenses for each category, with two modifications.

First, although there is a single expense standard for mortgage or rental expenses, our qualitative analyses suggested that the use of this standard might have very different effects on homeowners and renters. During the interviews, it was noted that, while renters must use the IRS expense standards for housing expenses regardless of their actual rent, homeowners get to deduct their entire mortgage payment. Some participants felt that the IRS expense standards favored owners. To address this concern, we divided the debtors in each of our samples into two groups: homeowners and renters. We then computed the difference between debtors' IRS mortgage or rental housing allowances and their corresponding current expenses for homeowners and for renters separately. Table 4.5 shows the numbers of homeowners and renters in our Chapter 13 sample for each of the districts.

Second, the IRS provides separate standards for the debtor's first and second cars. However, for simplicity, for debtors owning or leasing two cars, we considered only the combined IRS-related deductions for the first and second cars without distinguishing between the two.

Table 4.6 shows the average differences between the IRS expense standards and the debtors' corresponding current expenses for each of the IRS standard categories, modified as described previously.

The IRS standards for living expenses and for transportation ownership are generally favorable to debtors. In every sample district, the average IRS-related deductions in these two categories exceed the average corresponding current expenses. Part of the explanation for this difference is that the IRS standard for living expenses includes an allowance of $110 to $193, depending on family size, for miscellaneous expenses. There is no corresponding miscellaneous expense category on Schedule J, even though debtors likely do have actual, current, miscellaneous expenses.

Conversely, the IRS standard allowances for nonmortgage housing expenses and for vehicle operation and public transportation expenses are generally unfavorable to debtors. In every district, these calculations allow debtors lower deductions than their current expenses.

The rules for calculating the deduction for mortgage or rental expenses generally favor owners, though the differences between the deduction that owners are allowed using the IRS standards and their current expenses in that category are generally small, averaging $38 (Middle District of Florida) to $76 (Central District of California). The effects of the rules for calculating the deduction for mortgage or rental expenses using the IRS standards on renters are mixed. In five of the eight districts, the IRS standards result in smaller deductions, on average, than current expenses. In the other three districts, the average renter is allowed a larger IRS-related deduction in this category than his or her current expenses.

Table 4.5
Homeowners and Renters in Our Chapter 13 Samples

Judicial District	Owners	Renters
E.D.N.Y.	61	35
W.D. Tex.	82	18
W.D. Tenn.	67	26
N.D. Ohio	70	26
S.D. Iowa	75	24
C.D. Cal.	45	52
D. Utah	65	33
M.D. Fla.	62	32
All districts	527	246

Table 4.6
Difference Between IRS-Related Deductions and Corresponding Current Expenses

	Difference = IRS-Related Deduction – Corresponding Current Expenses ($)					
Judicial District	Living Expenses	Nonmortgage Housing Expenses	Mortgage or Rental Expenses (Owners)	Mortgage or Rental Expenses (Renters)	Vehicle Operation and Public Transportation Expenses	Transportation Ownership
E.D.N.Y.	399	–141	62	–25	–9	319
W.D. Tex.	428	–268	55	60	–114	336
W.D. Tenn.	370	–235	42	80	–109	348
N.D. Ohio	468	–244	52	–32	–63	422
S.D. Iowa	403	–250	41	–103	–69	313
C.D. Cal.	565	–298	76	–8	–63	307
D. Utah	462	–201	63	128	–47	286
M.D. Fla.	363	–248	38	–184	–115	350
All districts	433	–236	52	–13	–74	335

During the qualitative interviews, participants noted that the IRS expense standards do not take into account the condition or age of a debtor's home: The nonmortgage housing and utility allowance is the same for new and as for older homes. The suggestion was made that older homes need more maintenance and are more costly to heat or cool than are newer homes.

The IRS-related deductions for vehicle operation and public transportation expenses are also generally less than debtors' corresponding current expenses. Participants noted that commuting distance affects transportation costs, so the allowance may be too low for some debtors, particularly those who live in rural areas and typically have a longer commute. Another issue raised was that the IRS expense standards might not reflect the rising cost of fuel. Finally, as with home maintenance, several participants thought it problematic that the operating allowance is the same for new and old cars, even though an old car would have greater upkeep costs. Staff at the regional U.S. trustees' offices we visited told us that debtors with older vehicles (six years and older) are allowed an additional $200 per month to cover these operational expenses. However, Chapter 13 trustees in some districts may not be following this policy.

The IRS-related deduction for transportation ownership and lease expenses is favorable to debtors in every district. Vehicle owners are allowed to deduct the difference, if positive, between the IRS standard for transportation ownership and lease expenses and their car payments. Accordingly, some debtors who claim car payments are allowed deductions that they would not have received if their current expenses had been used to compute their MDIs. Participants in the qualitative interviews noted a bias against debtors who lease in comparison to those who own a vehicle.

In sum, debtors' MDIs are generally lower when calculated using the IRS expense standards than when calculated using debtors' corresponding current expenses for three reasons:

- The IRS standards for living expenses are substantially greater than debtors' corresponding current expenses.
- In calculating MDIs, the IRS standards allow a deduction for the difference, if positive, between the IRS standard for transportation ownership and the debtor's auto payment.
- In calculating MDIs, the IRS standards allow a deduction for the difference, if positive, between the IRS standard for mortgage or rental expense and the debtor's actual mortgage payment.

Effects of Using the IRS Standards on Different Types of Debtors and in Different Districts

Using the IRS expense standards instead of current expenses to calculate a debtor's MDI might affect some kinds of debtors more than others. Further, debtors in some districts might be systematically affected more or less than are comparable debtors in other districts. Several participants in the qualitative interviews noted certain rules under BAPCPA that favor debtors with large amounts of secured debt. Debtors with mortgages and car loans can deduct their full monthly payment, no matter how large, as a secured claim. If a debtor moves to a less expensive house to pay off bills, he or she has less secured debt and therefore a greater MDI. Several participants worried that, since BAPCPA allows deductions for all secured claims (such as houses and cars) regardless of the amount of the lien, there is a perverse incentive for debtors to increase their secured debt before filing for bankruptcy. This effect, however, is not due to the IRS standards. It flows instead from BAPCPA's separate allowance for secured debt.

We used multiple regression models to explore the extent to which the difference between a debtor's IRS-related deductions and his or her corresponding current expenses was related to the debtor's financial characteristics or to the district in which the debtor filed. The financial characteristics are included in the model for two reasons: (1) to determine whether the changes introduced by BAPCPA had a differential impact on debtors distinguished by their financial circumstances and (2) to control for differences in financial circumstances of those filing in different districts.

A Chapter 13 debtor provides detailed information on his or her financial profile. Specifically, the debtor reports seven attributes of his or her financial status:

- real property (real estate)
- personal property (other than real estate)
- outstanding debt on secured claims
- outstanding debt on priority, unsecured claims (claims that, by law, must be paid in full)
- outstanding debt on nonpriority, unsecured claims
- current income

- current expenditures.

Table 4.7 presents the financial characteristics of the debtors in our sample for each judicial district and for all districts combined.

However, in preliminary analyses, we noted that a number of debtors' financial attributes were highly correlated. Because it would be inappropriate to include highly correlated variables in the analyses, we had to exclude at least one of them. Based on preliminary analyses, we decided to exclude the debtors' real property and current expenditures.[4] While the correlations among the remaining financial attributes are, in some cases, moderate, the standard errors when each financial variable is entered alone in the model differ little from those in the full model.

Upon inspection of the distributions of the outcome and financial attribute variables, we detected 10 observations with extreme outlying values.[5] Coincidentally, half were in the sample of homeowners and half in the sample of renters. When these outliers were included in the models, they were identified from residual plots and, using Cook's distance criterion, were found to have had an undue influence on the models and not to fit the models well. While

Table 4.7
Debtors' Financial Circumstances ($K)

			Outstanding Debt				
Judicial District	Real Property	Personal Property	Secured Claims	Unsecured, Priority Claims	Unsecured, Nonpriority Claims	Current Income	Current Expenditures
E.D.N.Y.	307.9	34.7	223.61	2.9	46.3	5.5	4.5
W.D. Tex.	117.6	62.5	130.6	4.7	37.1	4.6	3.7
W.D. Tenn.	114.6	30.4	127.6	4.0	34.7	3.8	2.7
N.D. Ohio	118.7	29.7	127.8	2.8	43.7	4.2	3.2
S.D. Iowa	114.1	46.2	127.1	4.3	46.6	4.4	3.5
C.D. Cal.	259.6	47.6	202.4	6.7	46.3	5.8	4.7
D. Utah	127.0	35.9	138.8	8.7	48.1	4.6	3.8
M.D. Fla.	130.1	25.3	116.3	3.4	56.6	4.4	3.3
All districts	160.4	39.2	148.9	4.6	44.9	4.7	3.7

[4] We excluded two variables and, in each case, they were one of a pair of highly correlated variables—current income and current expenditures or real property and outstanding debt on secured claims—the correlations were 0.98 and 0.89, respectively. A common cutoff used in variable selection criteria when one is interested in explanation instead of prediction is correlation > 0.8 (with correspondingly high variance inflation factors) which suggests selecting a subset of the highly correlated variables. With correlations as high as were found here, the variables are giving much the same information.

[5] There are both high and low outliers, though they are more often high. They are identified as outliers based on having values more (usually much more) than three times the interquartile range (IQR) away from the first or fourth quartile on either the outcome or one of the financial predictor variables.

these outliers are valid observations in the population of bankruptcy cases, they are extreme cases. We chose to exclude them from the regression analysis to focus on the effect of the change in bankruptcy law on all but the most extreme cases. With the focus on nonextreme cases, the findings are robust to minor changes in the model specification.

Table 4.8 presents the results of two linear regressions, one for homeowners and the other for renters. Each regresses the difference between a debtor's deductions using the IRS standards and his or her deductions using current expenses instead on the district in which the debtor filed the case and the five attributes of the financial profile.

For both homeowners and renters, the results for the debtors' financial characteristics do not show significant differences in the effects of using the IRS standards rather than debtors' current expenses, except for the effect of a debtor's current monthly income. In general, higher-income debtors, whether homeowners or renters, gain less from the use of the IRS standards rather than their current expenses than do otherwise similar, lower-income debtors. For homeowners, the average difference in deductions calculated using the IRS standards rather than current expenses is about $70 less for each additional $1,000 in current monthly income. The effect of current monthly income on the difference in deductions is even larger for renters. For renters, the average difference in deductions calculated using the IRS standards rather than current expenses is about $175 lower for each additional $1,000 in current monthly income. This effect is significant for homeowners and highly significant for renters; there is less than one chance in 1,000 of observing the result we observed for renters by chance.

However, none of the coefficients on any of the other financial characteristics in either of the regressions is significant at the 95-percent level. The data offer no reason to believe that the use of the IRS standards instead of current expenses disproportionately affects a particular type of debtor, distinguished by his or her financial characteristics, except for debtors with high current monthly incomes.

Because every debtor is in one or another of the districts, we could not include all eight districts in the regression. Preliminary analyses showed that, controlling for debtors' financial characteristics, the debtors in the District of Utah tended to fall in the center of the distribution of differences between a debtor's deductions using the two alternative calculations. Accordingly, we chose to use the District of Utah as the base case in the final analysis. The coefficients on the other district variables show the amount by which, on average, the difference in deductions using the two expense calculations in those districts compares with the difference in the District of Utah for a debtor with the same financial characteristics. For example, the coefficient for the Eastern District of New York in the model of homeowners' differences is $229.81. This means that a homeowner in the Eastern District of New York with specified financial characteristics would have a difference in deductions according to the two calculations that is $230 larger, on average, than the difference between the two calculations for a homeowner with the same financial characteristics in the District of Utah. In other words, the difference between IRS standards and the corresponding current expenses is about $230 larger in the Eastern District of New York than in the District of Utah.

Table 4.8
Differential Effects of Using the IRS Standards, by Debtors' Judicial District and Financial Attributes

	Owners		Renters	
Attribute	**Estimated Coefficient**	**Standard Error**	**Estimated Coefficient**	**Standard Error**
Intercept	973.24[a]	105.35	1519.10[a]	143.89
Financial attribute ($ thousands)				
Personal property	0.39	0.63	0.00	0.49
Outstanding debt, secured claims	−0.53	0.34	−1.50	0.68
Outstanding debt, unsecured priority claims	1.19	3.26	−4.40	3.40
Outstanding debt, unsecured nonpriority claims	−0.69	0.64	0.80	1.44
Current monthly income	−69.68[b]	23.14	−175.30[a]	32.09
Judicial district				
E.D.N.Y.	229.81[b]	113.79	11.37	176.21
W.D. Tex.	−138.87	93.29	−234.53	166.98
W.D. Tenn.	−239.62[b]	99.67	−225.95	143.86
N.D. Ohio	25.54	91.29	−112.41	136.03
S.D. Iowa	−169.73	97.16	−339.44[b]	155.51
C.D. Cal.	352.63[b]	141.97	30.94	153.31
D. Utah	0.00	0.00	0.00	0.00
M.D. Fla.	−181.05	103.15	−589.47[a]	139.14
R2	0.13		0.32	
N	522		242	

[a] $p < 0.001$.
[b] $p < 0.05$.

There are substantial differences among the districts in the effects of using the IRS standards instead of the corresponding current expenses to calculate a debtor's deductions and, consequently, his or her MDI. The coefficients for homeowners range from a high of $353 in the Central District of California to a low of −$240 in the Western District of Tennessee, a difference of almost $600. The difference between a Central District of California homeowner's IRS-related deductions and his or her corresponding current expenses would be about $353 greater, on average, than the corresponding differences for a District of Utah homeowner who had the same financial characteristics. Controlling for financial characteristics, the difference between a Western District of Tennessee homeowner's deductions calculated using the IRS standards and his or her corresponding current expenses would be about $240 less, on average, than the corresponding differences for a District of Utah homeowner who had the same financial characteristics. Consequently, the average difference between a Central District of California homeowner's deductions calculated using the IRS standards and his or her deductions calculated using current expenses would be about $600 greater than the corresponding differences for a Western District of Tennessee homeowner who had the same financial characteristics.

In sum, the results presented in Table 4.8 imply that the effect on homeowners of using the IRS standards rather than current expenses to calculate deductions and, consequently, MDI, varies across the country.

The coefficients for renters also vary across the sample districts. They range from a high of $30.94 in the Central District of California to a low of –$589.47 in the Middle District of Florida, a difference of just over $600. The effect on renters of using the IRS standards rather than current expenses to calculate a debtor's deductions and, consequently, his or her MDI, also varies across the country.

The parameter estimates and related significance tests for a difference between each district and Utah are not of primary interest. To explore what the differences are between the districts, we tested each pairwise difference between districts. Table 4.9 presents F-tests of the significance of the difference between each pair of districts, controlling for financial characteristics.

We report two significance tests in the table. One adjusts for multiple testing. Because we have run 28 pairwise tests, to keep the type I error within the standard limits, we use a Bonferroni adjustment for the alpha level for each test. Instead of using a 0.05 cutoff for significance, we use a cutoff of 0.05/28 = 0.0018. This is a conservative adjustment, but not adjusting leads to greater type I error. The other test is the standard test of significance at the 0.05 level without adjusting for multiple testing.

We can reject the hypothesis that there are no differences among districts for homeowners. Controlling for debtors' financial circumstances, the differences for homeowners in the Central District of California are significantly different at the 0.05 level from the differences for homeowners in six of the other seven districts. Controlling for debtors' financial circumstances, the differences for homeowners in each of the other districts each significantly differ from three to five of the other districts.

There are some, but fewer, significant differences among districts for renters. Controlling for debtors' financial circumstances, the differences for renters in the Middle District of Florida and the Central District of California are significantly different from those in four and three other districts, respectively. None of the other six districts exhibits significant differences from more than two other districts.

We reran the regressions using all the financial predictors or the alternate predictors in the two problematic pairs—real property and outstanding debt on secured claims and current income and current expenditures. For owners, the results of both of these alternate specifications were very similar to the model presented—neither variable from the real property and outstanding debt on secured claims pair was ever significant, and current expenditures was significant

Table 4.9
Significance of Interdistrict Differences

	Owners		Renters	
Contrast	**F Value**	**p > F**	**F Value**	**p > F**
California versus Florida	14.54[a]	0.0002	13.56[a]	0.0003
California versus Iowa	12.51[a]	0.0004	3.96[b]	0.0478
California versus New York	0.26	0.6077	0.64	0.4247
California versus Ohio	5.18[b]	0.0233	0.56	0.4538
California versus Tennessee	18.96[a]	<0.0001	5.12[b]	0.0245
California versus Texas	11.33[a]	0.0008	1.83	0.1773
California versus Utah	5.21[b]	0.0228	0.01	0.9059
Florida versus Iowa	1.05	0.3060	2.45	0.1189
Florida versus New York	17.46[a]	<0.0001	4.33[b]	0.0384
Florida versus Ohio	8.51[b]	0.0037	12.52[a]	0.0005
Florida versus Tennessee	0.01	0.9312	1.08	0.3007
Florida versus Texas	2.19	0.1396	4.62	0.0325
Florida versus Utah	6.07[b]	0.0140	16.72[a]	<0.0001
Iowa versus New York	14.53[a]	0.0002	0.74	0.3912
Iowa versus Ohio	4.51[b]	0.0341	2.36	0.1255
Iowa versus Tennessee	1.32	0.2512	0.18	0.6729
Iowa versus Texas	0.29	0.5876	0.34	0.5608
Iowa versus Utah	2.75	0.0976	4.48[b]	0.0354
New York versus Ohio	5.10	0.0244	0.06	0.8007
New York versus Tennessee	21.52[a]	<0.0001	1.34	0.2486
New York versus Texas	12.93[a]	0.0004	0.13	0.7214
New York versus Utah	5.07[b]	0.0248	0.57	0.4521
Ohio versus Tennessee	9.71[b]	0.0019	3.58	0.0598
Ohio versus Texas	2.91	0.0888	0.62	0.4322
Ohio versus Utah	0.04	0.8414	0.56	0.4564
Tennessee versus Texas	2.91	0.0885	0.91	0.3414
Tennessee versus Utah	6.95[b]	0.0086	6.21[b]	0.0134
Texas versus Utah	1.54	0.2152	1.90	0.1697

[a] Significant after adjusting for multiple testing.

[b] Significant without adjusting for multiple testing.

only in the model that excluded current income. The other model estimates were very similar (including which state differences were significant) except for marked increases in the standard errors of the pair variables when both variables in each pair were included. For the renters, including both property and outstanding debt on secured claims or replacing outstanding debt on secured claims with real property caused the variable(s) representing this pair to lose statistical significance (which was not strong in the model presented). The effects on the other pair mirrored those in the owner model and, again, the effects on other model estimates were minor. Overall, the differences in the model results under these various specifications are minor.

CHAPTER FIVE

Summary and Conclusions

Our analyses of the effects of using the IRS expense standards to calculate a debtor's MDI focused on six questions.

How Have the Court Rulings Affected the Use of IRS Standards in Calculating a Debtor's MDI and to What Extent Has This Use Affected Bankruptcy Courts' Workload?

The use of IRS expense standards as part of the means test has resulted in many questions related to statutory interpretation, and bankruptcy courts have frequently disagreed. BAPCPA took effect too recently for appellate courts to have had time to settle the many open questions. As a result, there is nonuniformity among judicial districts in application of the IRS standards in Chapter 7 and Chapter 13. These differences of opinion mean that similarly situated debtors may have substantially different payment obligations depending on the jurisdiction in which they live. The differing burden of payment among the jurisdictions is likely to produce disparities in the relative proportions of Chapter 7 versus Chapter 13 cases as well as in rate of confirmation and completion of Chapter 13 plans among similarly situated debtors.

In August 2006, the AO reported on BAPCPA's impact on the federal judiciary. BAPCPA created more than 35 new types of motions, objections, and hearings that did not previously exist. Most judges seem to agree that each case now requires more of their time, but the effects seem to vary greatly depending upon the district. Some judges report a marked increase in workload due to BAPCPA, but others report few to no new problems. The AO report does not attribute an increase in workload to a particular provision of the new law; therefore, what portion may be due to the IRS expense standards is not known.

Some of our interview participants noted that the number of motions filed in their districts had decreased, mirroring the decrease in the number of bankruptcy cases filed post-BAPCPA. Others reported that there have been more motions filed since the law was passed, especially around the issue of vehicle expenses.

What Fraction of Chapter 7 Filers Had Above-Median Incomes but Satisfied the Chapter 7 Presumption Because Their MDIs Satisfied the Means Test?

Overall, about 7 percent of the Chapter 7 debtors had above-median incomes but could file under Chapter 7 because their total deductions met the relevant Chapter 7 criteria. There was noticeable variation across judicial districts in the fraction of Chapter 7 filers who had above-median incomes. Our sample of debtors who filed for Chapter 7 in the Central District of California did not include a single above-median–income debtor; thus, no Chapter 7 cases in our sample from the Central District of California used the IRS expense standards to escape the presumption of abuse for a Chapter 7 filing. However, in each of the other districts, some above-median–income debtors had total deductions, including those calculated using IRS standards, that resulted in MDIs below the abuse thresholds. In brief, the effects of the means test, including the use of the IRS standards, on would-be Chapter 7 filers is very uneven, substantial in some parts of the country and inconsequential in others.

We have no way to determine the number of above-median–income debtors who would have filed under Chapter 7 but did not because their MDI calculated using the IRS expense standards did not escape the presumption of abuse and either filed under Chapter 13 or never filed at all. Consequently, we cannot estimate the fraction of would-be Chapter 7 filers who were affected by the means test in the sense that they were precluded from filing under Chapter 7. Similarly, we cannot estimate the extent to which the use of the IRS allowances permitted more debtors to qualify for Chapter 7 protection than if current expenses had been used.

To What Degree Did Use of the IRS Standards Affect Debtors Who Filed for Chapter 13?

Overall, almost three-quarters of the debtors who filed under Chapter 13 had below-median incomes. These debtors presumably could have filed under Chapter 7, but opted for a Chapter 13 filing instead. During the qualitative discussions, participants reported as reasons that debtors eligible for Chapter 7 protection might file under Chapter 13 such things as increased attorney's fees, the responsibility-to-pay culture in certain districts, and the desire to halt foreclosure on a home.

There was substantial variation across judicial districts in the fraction of Chapter 13 filers whose income exceeded the median and, consequently, had to use the IRS standards to calculate their MDIs. The proportion of above-median–income debtors who used the IRS standards when filing under Chapter 13 in the Eastern District of New York, the Western District of Texas, the Southern District of Iowa, and the Central District of California was well above the average for all sample districts in each case.

At the other extreme, only 13 percent of the Chapter 13 debtors in the Western District of Tennessee had above-median incomes and, consequently, used the IRS expense standards to calculate their MDIs. Presumably, all of these below-median–income debtors and some of the above-median–income debtors who filed under Chapter 13 in this judicial district could have filed under Chapter 7 but chose not to do so. The qualitative interviews revealed that this district has an historical culture of using Chapter 13 rather than Chapter 7 even if the filer has low means.

We cannot observe above-median–income debtors who wished to file under Chapter 13, used the IRS standards in computing their MDIs, and, because they thought that their MDIs would not give them enough flexibility to have a feasible plan, did not file. Consequently, we have no data on the extent to which the IRS standards deterred a would-be Chapter 13 filer.

For Above-Median–Income, Chapter 13 Filers, How Does MDI Calculated Using Current Expenses Compare with MDI Calculated Using IRS Standards?

The use of IRS standards rather than current expenses to calculate MDI results in a lower MDI, on average, in every one of the sample districts and in all districts combined. On average, MDI is reduced by $490 in all districts combined when the IRS standards are used. In individual districts, the average reduction due to the use of the IRS standards ranges from $311 in the Middle District of Florida to $612 in the Northern District of Ohio. Across the country, the IRS standards result in larger deductions, on average, and, therefore, lower MDIs.

Some debtors in each district had IRS-related deductions that were less than their corresponding current expenses. For these debtors, the difference between the two calculations is negative. The percentage of such debtors ranges from 9 percent in the Northern District of Ohio to 21 percent in the Central District of California.

The IRS standards clearly allow debtors higher deductions for living expenses, on average, than debtors claim are their current living expenses. In part, this results from the IRS's miscellaneous allowance of $110 to $193, which has no corresponding Schedule J current expense. Conversely, on average, the IRS standards allow debtors much smaller deductions for nonmortgage housing expenses and vehicle operating expenses than debtors' corresponding current expenses.

During the qualitative interviews, it was suggested that renters did not fare as well as homeowners when using the IRS expense standards. In fact, our analysis shows that the IRS standard for mortgage or rental expenses is generally more favorable to homeowners than to renters. The deduction allowed homeowners for the difference, if positive, between the IRS standard for mortgage or rental expenses and their mortgage payment is always positive, though generally not very large. The effect of the IRS standard for mortgage or rental expenses on renters is mixed. In five of the eight sample districts, the IRS allows renters smaller deductions, on average, than their rent payments. But, in three districts, the reverse is true. Overall, for renters in all districts, on average, the weighted difference is only –$13.

For Above-Median–Income, Chapter 13 Filers, What, If Any, Financial Factors Are Systematically Related to the Difference Between MDI Calculated Using Current Expenses and MDI Calculated Using IRS Expense Standards?

Interview participants noted that debtors with mortgages and car loans could take the full deduction for the loan as a secured claim regardless of how large the loan. Debtors who do not have these expenses, however, must use the IRS expense standards, which limit their expenses and leave them with more disposable income. Therefore, debtors with large amounts of secured debt have less disposable income to use to pay back creditors, whereas debtors with little or no secured debt have more disposable income available to pay creditors.

However, the empirical results for the debtor's financial characteristics do not show significant differences in the effects of using the IRS standards, except for debtors with high current income. In general, higher-income debtors gain less using the IRS standards rather than their current expenses than do otherwise similar, lower-income debtors. For homeowners, the difference in deductions calculated using the IRS standards rather than current expenses is, on average, about $70 lower for each $1,000 in current monthly income. For renters, the difference in deductions calculated using the IRS standards rather than current expenses is, on average, about $175 lower for each $1,000 in current monthly income. This effect is significant for homeowners and highly significant for renters.

None of the other financial characteristics has a significant effect on debtors' MDIs. The data offer no reason to believe that the use of the IRS standards instead of current expenses disfavors a particular type of debtor, distinguished by his or her financial characteristics, except for debtors with high current income.

For Above-Median–Income, Chapter 13 Filers, Do Patterns in the Differences Between MDI Calculated Using Current Expenses and MDI Calculated Using IRS Expense Standards Differ Across Judicial Districts?

The results for the judicial districts suggest that, controlling for debtors' financial characteristics, there are some systematic differences among the districts in the effects of using the IRS standards instead of the corresponding current expenses to calculate a debtor's MDI. The district effect is more pronounced for owners than for renters. Controlling for debtors' financial circumstances, the differences for homeowners in each of the other districts vary significantly from three to five of the other districts.

There are some, but many fewer, significant differences among districts for renters.

APPENDIX

Office Focus Group Discussion Guide

Introduction (2 min)

Welcome. Thank you for coming to this group discussion. I'm {NAME} from the RAND Corporation, a nonprofit research institution, in (Washington, D.C./Santa Monica, California). [With me are {NAMES}].

RAND is conducting an important study on behalf of the Executive Office of the United States Trustees (EOUST) to evaluate the impact of changes in the Bankruptcy Abuse Prevention and Consumer Protection Act of 2005 (BAPCPA). To this end, the RAND research team is conducting two separate studies for EOUST. One evaluates the effect of using the IRS standards in determining current monthly expenses of above-median–income debtors and whether or not using this standard is having an effect on bankruptcy courts. The other seeks to quantify the impact of the new definition of *household goods exemptions* provided by BAPCPA on business practices, debtors, and the courts. We are conducting this group discussion with support from the Executive Office for United States Trustees. We are holding these discussions so that we will have a better understanding of the effect of changes brought about by BAPCPA on debtors.

We are audiotaping today's discussion. The tapes will be transcribed and we will destroy the tapes as soon as the transcripts are completed. The transcripts will be shared with EOUST.

Ground Rules (3 min)

In order to make the best use of your time, I'd like to go over a few ground rules before we begin.

First, we want to hear from everyone. Please treat this as a discussion; ask questions of each other, and respond to what others are saying, whether you agree or disagree.

- Feel free to ask for clarification if you did not understand a question.
- Your participation is entirely voluntary. You should feel free to skip any topic or leave the group at any time.
- Finally, there are no right or wrong answers. Please give us your honest opinions. We're here to learn from you.

We have quite a few topics to cover, so I may use a "time out" sign if I need to move the discussion to another topic. Are there any questions? May we begin?

Group Introduction

I'd like to go around the table starting on my right and to have each person tell us just your first name and how long you have been working here and your role in the office.

Topic:
IRS Expense Allowance Standards
(20 min)

One of the main changes in the Bankruptcy Abuse Prevention and Consumer Protection Act of 2005 (BAPCPA) was the application of the IRS expense allowance standards to above-median–income filers. I want to begin by discussing what effects the use of the IRS expense allowance standards has had on above-median–income filers.

1. What kind of changes have you seen due to the application of the IRS expense allowance standards to above-median–income filers? For instance, are you seeing more people being shifted to Chapter 13 from Chapter 7 or vice versa? Is this because of the IRS expense allowance standards?
2. Are you seeing more people in Chapter 7 with means to pay due to the high median income in this area?
3. If a debtor is above median income and wants to file for Chapter 7, what is the process used to determine their eligibility?
4. Are Schedule I or J used at all in the process? If so, how?
5. What forms are you seeing debtors' attorneys using to calculate disposable income?
6. What role, if any, do Schedules I and J now play in your jurisdiction where section 707(b) is concerned?
7. What types of situations are debtors asking the court to recognize as special circumstances under 707(b) in your district? Which of these has the court or have you decided do, in fact, qualify as special circumstances? Do any involve expenses that the IRS allowances cover at least in part?
8. Do the IRS expense allowance standards seem to adequately reflect the debtor's actual expenses? How do these expenses differ from those in Schedule J?
9. Do people underestimate their expenses? What kinds of expenses do they underestimate?
10. How are the IRS expense allowances working in practice? What is actually deductible?
11. How are paid-off cars dealt with in your jurisdiction? What type of allowance do petitioners with paid-off cars receive? (Do they receive the full ownership allowance—or something else?)
12. What about the transportation allowance: Has this been adequate? What about for a debtor who owns a car but also uses public transportation?
13. How should debtors treat auto ownership allowances if they say on the statement of intention that they will surrender one or more vehicles? Does it make a difference whether they intend to replace the surrendered car ASAP? What about if they are intending to surrender a home?
14. What about costs for rental expenses? Are those adequate?
15. Does any one of the IRS fixed-dollar allowances cause more controversy or difficulty than the others in your district? Why?
16. Did you field many questions from attorneys and trustees related to the interpretation of this new part of the law? What types of questions?

Topic:
Courts
(5 min)

1. What effect, if any, do you think use of the IRS expense allowance standards has had on the bankruptcy courts? (More motions? Fewer motions?)
2. Is there less time or more time spent deciding on expenses since BAPCPA?
3. Are there other effects?
4. IF EFFECTS: Do you think this is just because BAPCPA is a new law, or are there specific problems with using the IRS expense allowances in calculating current monthly expenses?

Topic:
Household Goods
(10 min)

Next, I want to discuss the new definition of *household goods* provided by BAPCPA on business practices.

1. Have you noticed any changes by businesses in their practices since BAPCPA? For instance, have you seen a difference in the type of household goods used to secure the claims? For instance, have you seen liens against household goods that are no longer exempt?
2. Have you seen a difference in the total amount and/or number of claims against the debtor that are secured by household goods?
3. What effect, if any, do you think the changes in the exemptions on household goods have had on the bankruptcy courts? (More motions? Fewer motions?) (FOLLOW UP WITH ADDITIONAL COURT QUESTIONS IF NEEDED.)
4. Who do you think this change is affecting? Why was this change made to the law?
5. Do you know of any companies that extend credit by using household goods to secure the claim?
6. Are you aware of the FTC law affecting loans on household goods?

Topic: Implementation (10 min)	1. How was it to implement the new rules? 2. Did you field many questions from attorneys and trustees related to interpretation of the new law (e.g., where to find the IRS tables, or the U.S. trustee's position on certain types of allowances)? 3. What kinds of questions did you have to answer? 4. Did you feel prepared to answer or give advice to attorneys and trustees? What types of preparation or training did you receive? 5. What about others with whom you had to work (e.g., trustees, courts)? Were they up to date with the new procedures?
Additional Thoughts (5 min)	Is there something we didn't cover about changes in the bankruptcy law that you think we should have included in this discussion? If you have any other thoughts or comments, please feel free to talk to me after the group.
Thank you (1 min)	That's the end of my questions. Thanks very much for taking part in this discussion today; it was very helpful to us.

References

Administrative Office of the U.S. Courts, *Report on the Impact of the Bankruptcy Abuse Prevention and Consumer Protection Act of 2005 on the Workload of the Federal Judiciary*, Washington, D.C.: Administrative Office of the U.S. Courts, August 2006. As of April 26, 2007: http://www.abiworld.org/am/Template.cfm?Section=What_s_New_Top_Items&Template=/CM/ContentDisplay.cfm&ContentID=42657

AO—*see* Administrative Office of the U.S. Courts.

Baxter v. Johnson (In re Johnson), 346 B.R. 256, Bankr. S.D. Ga., July 21, 2006.

In re Alexander, 344 B.R. 742, Bankr. E.D.N.C., August 23, 2006.

In re Barraza, 346 B.R. 724, Bankr. N.D. Tex. 2006.

In re Demonica, 345 B.R. 895, Bankr. N.D. Ill., July 31, 2006.

In re Diagostino, 347 B.R. 116, Bankr. N.D.N.Y., August 28, 2006.

In re Farrar-Johnson, 353 B.R. 224, Bankr. N.D. Ill., September 15, 2006.

In re Fowler, 349 B.R. 414, Bankr. D. Del., September 11, 2006.

In re Fuller, 346 B.R. 472, Bankr. S.D. Ill., June 21, 2006.

In re Guzman, 345 B.R. 640, Bankr. E.D. Wis., July 19, 2006.

In re Haley, 354 B.R. 340, Bankr. D.N.H., October 18, 2006.

In re Hardacre, 338 B.R. 718, Bankr. N.D. Tex., March 6, 2006.

In re Hartwick, 352 B.R. 867, Bankr. D. Minn., October 13, 2006.

In re Lara, 347 B.R. 198, Bankr. N.D. Tex., June 28, 2006.

In re McGuire, 342 B.R. 608, Bankr. W.D. Mo., June 1, 2006.

In re Meyer, 355 B.R. 837, Bankr. D.N.M., December 4, 2006.

In re Oliver, 2006 WL 2086691, Bankr. D. Or., June 29, 2006.

In re Ray, 2007 WL 690131, Bankr. D.S.C., February 28, 2007.

In re Risher, 344 B.R. 833, Bankr. W.D. Ky., July 12, 2006.

In re Slusher, 2007 WL 118009, Bankr. D. Nev., January 17, 2007.

In re Tranmer, 355 B.R. 234, Bankr. D. Mont., November 16, 2006.

In re Walker, 2006 WL 1314125, Bankr. N.D. Ga., May 1, 2006.

In re Wiggs, 2006 WL 2246432, Bankr. N.D. Ill., August 4, 2006.

In re Wilson, 356 B.R. 114, Bankr. D. Del., December 11, 2006.

Internal Revenue Manual, Washington, D.C.: U.S. Department of the Treasury, Internal Revenue Service, quarterly since 1997.

Internal Revenue Service, "Collection Financial Standards," undated Web page. As of April 2, 2007: http://www.irs.gov/individuals/article/0,,id=96543,00.html

IRS—*see* Internal Revenue Service.

Public Law 109-8, Bankruptcy Abuse Prevention and Consumer Protection Act of 2005, April 20, 2005. As of April 2, 2007:
http://frwebgate.access.gpo.gov/cgi-bin/getdoc.cgi?dbname=109_cong_public_laws&docid=f:publ008.109

Public Law 109-439, Religious Liberty and Charitable Donation Clarification Act of 2006, December 20, 2006.

White, Clifford J., III, director, Executive Office for U.S. Trustees, *Oversight of the Implementation of the Bankruptcy Abuse Prevention and Consumer Protection Act*, testimony before the Subcommittee on Administrative Oversight of the Courts, Committee on the Judiciary, U.S. Senate, December 6, 2006.